Quick & Easy
Simple Thai

p

Contents

Introduction..4
Thai-style Seafood Soup......................................6
Chicken & Coconut Soup.....................................7
Cold Coriander Soup...8
Thai Fish Soup...9
Sweetcorn & Crab Soup.....................................10
Pumpkin & Coconut Soup..................................11
Mushroom & Tofu Broth.....................................12
Rice Soup with Eggs...13
Spinach & Ginger Soup......................................14
Chilled Avocado Soup...15
Prawn Satay...16
Sweet & Sour Fish Cakes...................................17
Thai Noodles...18
Fish Cakes with Hot Sauce................................19
Thai-style Crab Sandwich..................................20
Sticky Ginger Chicken Wings.............................21
Lemon Grass Chicken...22
Thai Stuffed Omelette..23
Thai-spiced Sausages...24
Thai-style Burgers..25
Hot & Sour Noodles...26
Pad Thai Noodles..27
Rice Noodles & Mushrooms...............................28
Drunken Noodles..29
Rice Noodles with Chicken.................................30
Stir-fried Pork with Pasta..................................31
Pad Thai Noodles..32
Stir-fried Beef...33
Beef Satay..34
Beef, Peppers & Lemon Grass...........................35
Hot Beef & Coconut Curry.................................36
Roasted Red Pork..37
Pork with Sesame Seeds....................................38

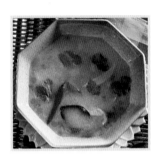

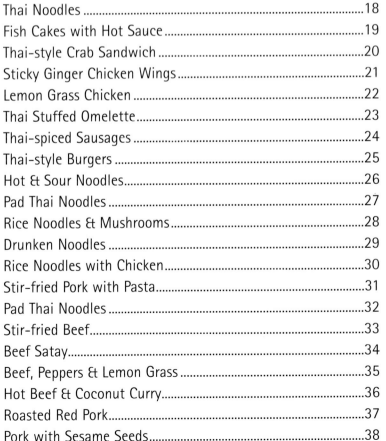

Spicy Fried Minced Pork 39

Red Lamb Curry...40

Chicken & Mango Stir-Fry 41

Thai Coriander Chicken...42

Green Chicken Curry...43

Glazed Duck Breasts 44

Crispy Duck with Noodles 45

Thai Green Fish Curry 46

Red Prawn Curry..47

Coconut Rice & Monkfish 48

Steamed Yellow Fish Fillets 49

Baked Fish with Chilli Sauce 50

Curry-coated Baked Cod 51

Sweet & Sour Tuna 52

Thai-spiced Salmon..53

Salmon with Red Curry...54

Squid with Hot Sauce 55

Scallops with Lime & Chilli 56

Spicy Prawn Skewers..57

Thai Potato Stir-Fry..58

Thai-style Caesar Salad 59

Thai Noodle & Prawn Salad 60

Thai Seafood Salad...61

Warm Tuna Salad 62

Egg Noodle & Turkey Salad 63

Jasmine Rice 64

Coconut Rice with Pineapple..65

Vegetables in Peanut Sauce 66

Thai Red Bean Curry..67

Stir-fried Vegetables...68

Broccoli in Oyster Sauce 69

Spiced Cashew Nut Curry 70

Potato & Spinach Curry 71

Crispy Tofu with Chilli Sauce...72

Mango & Lemon Grass Syrup 73

Exotic Fruit Salad 74

Rose Ice 75

Lychee & Ginger Sorbet...76

Cardamom & Lime Pineapple 77

Bananas in Coconut Milk..78

Thai Rice Pudding..79

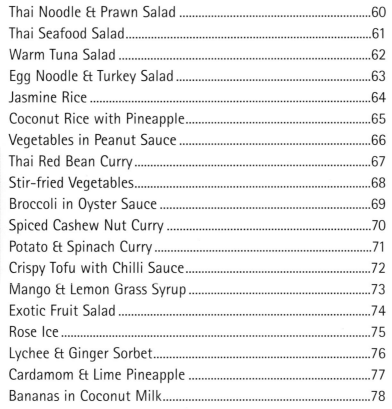

Introduction

Anyone who loves Thai food will appreciate that it is a unique cuisine, distinctly different from the cooking of the countries which border it, but with many culinary influences from far beyond its geographical frontiers. Thai cooking owes many of its characteristics to climate and culture, but a history of many centuries of invasions and emigration has played a large part in shaping its cuisine. The roots of the Thai nation can be traced back to the first century, the time of the Chinese Han Dynasty, when the T'ai tribes occupied parts of South China along valuable trade routes between the East and the West. Over the years, the T'ai had a close but often stormy relationship with the Chinese, and eventually began to emigrate south to the lands of what is now northern Thailand, bordering Burma and Cambodia, then sparsely occupied by Buddhist and Hindu communities.

In time, the T'ai established the independent Kingdom of Sukhothai (translated as 'dawn of happiness'), which eventually became Siam. The ports of Siam were the entrance to an important trade route, and ships from all over Europe and Japan docked there, or sailed inland along the rivers, bringing foreign foods, teas, spices, silks, copper and ceramics. In the 16th century, the Portuguese introduced the chilli to South East Asia. The

plant flourished immediately in the region's soils and climates, and continues to thrive. Trade with Arab and Indian merchants was important, and many Muslims settled in Siam.

The Kingdom of Siam survived until 1939, when it became the constitutional Thai monarchy, and 21st-century Thailand still reflects much of her past centuries of mixed cultures. The Thai people are independent, proud, creative and passionate. Their love of life is apparent in the way they take pleasure in entertaining and eating. They seem to a visitor to eat all day long. The streets and waterways are lined with food vendors selling a huge variety of tasty snacks from their stalls, carts, bicycles and boats, all day long.

Thai people love parties and celebrations, and during their many festivals, the colourful, often elaborate and carefully prepared festive foods show a respect for custom and tradition. Visitors are entertained with an unending succession of trays of tasty snacks, platters of exotic fruits, and Thai beer, or local whisky. When a meal is served, all the dishes are served together, so the cook can enjoy the food along with the guests.

Thais take pride in presenting food beautifully. They carve vegetables and fruit into elaborate shapes as garnishes. Their intricate patterns and skilled artistry are an integral part of Thai culture, which exhibits a deep appreciation of beautiful things..

Everyday life in Thailand is closely tied to the seasons, marked by the harvesting of crops and the vagaries of the monsoon climate. The Thai people take food seriously, exercizing great care in choosing the freshest of ingredients, and thoughtfully balancing delicate flavours and textures. Throughout Thailand, rice is the most important staple food, the centre of every meal. And coconut, in its various forms, has an almost equal place. Cooks in every region are expert at making the most of any ingredient available locally, so the character of many classic Thai dishes will vary according to the region in which they are cooked.

Fundamentals of Thai Cooking

The essential ingredients you need to have in order to cook Thai food are listed below. Of these, the most important are coconut, lime, chilli, rice, garlic, lemon grass, ginger root and coriander. With these you can create many traditional Thai dishes. Although many recipes have long lists of ingredients, the cooking methods involved in making them are simple enough even for inexperienced cooks to follow .

Balance is the guiding principle of Thai cooking, the five extremes of flavour - bitter, sour, hot, salt, and sweet - being carefully and skillfully balanced in each dish and over several courses. Every dish therefore contributes to the balance of the entire meal.

Basil Three varieties of sweet basil are used in Thai cooking, but the variety commonly sold in the West also works well. Oriental food stores often sell the seeds for Thai basil, so you can grow your own.

Chillies The many varieties of chilli vary in heat from very mild to fiery hot, so choose carefully. The small red or green bird-eye chillies are often used in Thai dishes. They are very hot, and if you prefer a mild heat you should remove the seeds. Red chillies are generally slightly sweeter and milder than green. Larger chillies tend to be milder. Dried crushed chillies are used for seasoning.

Coconut Milk This is made from grated, pressed fresh coconut. It is sold very widely in cans and longlife packs, in powdered form, and in blocks as creamed coconut. Coconut cream is skimmed from the top, and is slightly thicker and richer.

Coriander This is a fresh herb with a pungent, citrus-like flavour, widely used in savoury dishes. It wilts quite quickly, so retains its freshness best if bought with a root attached. Alternatively, you can grow your own. It will make a difference to your cooking.

Galangal A relative of ginger, with a milder, aromatic flavour. Galangal is available fresh or dried.

Garlic The pungent cloves of this bulb are used abundantly in Thai cooking. It us used whole, crushed, sliced, or chopped, in savoury dishes and curry pastes. Fresh garlic can be bought widely, but pickled garlic is a useful purchase because it makes an attractive garnish.

Ginger

Fresh ginger root is peeled and grated, chopped or sliced for a warm, spicy flavour.

Kaffir Lime Leaves

These leaves have a distinctive lime scent, and can be bought fresh, dried or frozen.

Lemon Grass

An aromatic tropical grass with a lemon scent similar to lemon balm. Strip off the fibrous outer leaves and slice or chop the insides finely, or bruise and use whole. Lemon grass can also be bought in dried powdered form.

Palm Sugar

This is a rich, brown unrefined sugar made from the coconut palm and sold in solid blocks. The best way to use it is to crush it with a mallet or rolling pin. Muscovado sugar is a good substitute.

Rice Vinegar

Mirin, or sweet rice vinegar, is a savoury flavouring. Sherry or white wine vinegar can be substituted.

Soy Sauce

Dark and light soy sauce iare used for seasoning. The light sauce is saltier than the dark and is used mainly in stir-fries and with light meats. Dark soy adds a mature. rich flavour and colour to braised and red meat dishes.

Tamarind Paste

The pulp of the tamarind fruit is usually sold in blocks. It gives a sour/sweet flavour. Soak the pulp in hot water for 30 minutes, press out the juice and discard pulp and seeds.

Thai Fish Sauce

Called *nam pla,* this is used like salt for seasoning, and has a distinctive, intense aroma. It is made from salted fermented fish.

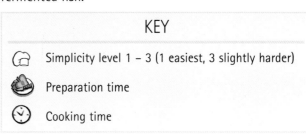

KEY

Simplicity level 1 – 3 (1 easiest, 3 slightly harder)

Preparation time

Cooking time

Thai-style Seafood Soup

Because taste and tolerance for chillies vary, it is best to use chilli purée. It enables you to control the level of the heat in the dish.

NUTRITIONAL INFORMATION

Calories	132	Sugars 7g
Protein	........20g	Fat 2g
Carbohydrate	....9g	Saturates 0.1g

 10–15 mins   25 mins

SERVES 4

INGREDIENTS

1.2 litres/2 pints fish stock

1 lemon grass stalk, split lengthways

pared rind of ½ lime, or 1 lime leaf

2.5 cm/1 inch piece fresh ginger root, peeled and sliced

¼ tsp chilli purée, or to taste

4–6 spring onions, sliced

200 g/7 oz large of medium raw prawns, peeled

250 g/9 oz scallops (16–20)

2 tbsp fresh coriander leaves

salt

finely chopped red pepper, or red chilli rings, to garnish

1 Put the stock in a saucepan with the lemon grass, lime rind or leaf, ginger and chilli purée. Bring just to the boil, reduce the heat, cover and simmer for 10–15 minutes.

2 Cut the baby leek in half lengthways, then slice crossways very thinly. Cut the prawns almost in half lengthways, keeping the tail intact.

3 Strain the stock, return to the saucepan and bring to a simmer, with bubbles rising at the edges and the surface trembling. Add the leek and cook for 2–3 minutes. Season with salt, if needed, and stir in more chilli purée if wished.

4 Add the scallops and prawns and poach for about 1 minute until they turn opaque and the prawns curl.

5 Drop in the fresh coriander leaves, ladle the soup into four warm bowls, dividing the shellfish evenly, and garnish the soup with red pepper or red chilli rings.

COOK'S TIP

If you have light chicken stock, but no fish stock, the chicken stock will make an equally tasty though different version of this soup.

Chicken & Coconut Soup

Make this soup when you want a change from traditional chicken soup. It is nicely spiced and garnished with coriander leaves.

NUTRITIONAL INFORMATION

Calories ....76 Sugars 2g
Protein ....13g Fat 1g
Carbohydrate ....3g Saturates 0.1g

15 mins   40–45 mins

SERVES 4

INGREDIENTS

1.2 litres/2 pints chicken stock

200 g/7 oz skinless boned chicken

1 fresh chilli, split lengthways
  and deseeded

7.5 cm/3 inch piece lemon grass,
  split lengthways

3–4 lime leaves

2.5 cm/1 inch piece fresh ginger root,
  peeled and sliced

120 ml/4 fl oz coconut milk

6–8 spring onions, sliced diagonally

¼ tsp chilli purée, or to taste

salt

fresh coriander leaves, to garnish

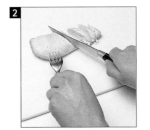

1 Put the stock in a pan with the chicken, chilli, lemon grass, lime leaves and ginger. Bring almost to the boil, reduce the heat, cover and simmer for 20–25 minutes, or until the chicken is cooked through and firm to the touch.

2 Remove the chicken and strain the stock. When the chicken is cool, slice thinly or shred into bite-sized pieces.

3 Return the stock to the saucepan and heat to simmering. Stir in the coconut milk and spring onions. Add the chicken and continue simmering for about 10 minutes, until the soup is heated through and the flavours have mingled.

4 Stir in the chilli purée. Season to taste with salt and, if wished, add a little more chilli purée.

5 Ladle the soup into warm bowls and float a few fresh coriander leaves on the surface of the soup to serve.

COOK'S TIP

Once the stock is flavoured and the chicken cooked, this soup is very quick to finish. If you wish, poach the chicken and strain the stock ahead of time. Store in the refrigerator separately.

Cold Coriander Soup

This soup brings together Thai flavours for a cool, refreshing starter. It highlights fresh coriander, now very widely available.

NUTRITIONAL INFORMATION

Calories 79	Sugars 5g	
Protein 3g	Fat 3g	
Carbohydrate . . .13g	Saturates 0.1g	

 10 mins   35–40 mins

SERVES 4

I N G R E D I E N T S

2 tsp olive oil

1 large onion, finely chopped

1 leek, thinly sliced

1 garlic clove, thinly sliced

1 litre/1¾ pints water

1 courgette, about 200 g/7 oz, peeled and chopped

4 tbsp white rice

5 cm/2 inch piece lemon grass

2 lime leaves

60 g/2 oz fresh coriander leaves and soft stems

chilli puree (optional)

salt and pepper

finely chopped red pepper and/or red chillies, to garnish

1 Heat the oil in a large saucepan over a medium heat. Add the onion, leek and garlic, cover and cook for 4–5 minutes until the onion is softened, stirring frequently.

2 Add the water, courgette and rice with a large pinch of salt and some pepper. Stir in the lemon grass and lime leaves. Bring to the boil and reduce the heat to low. Cover and simmer for about 15–20 minutes until the rice is soft and tender.

3 Add the fresh coriander leaves, pushing them down into the liquid. Continue cooking for 2–3 minutes until they are wilted. Remove the lemon grass and lime leaves.

4 Allow the soup to cool slightly, then transfer to a blender or food processor and purée until smooth.

5 Scrape the soup into a large container. Season to taste with salt and pepper. Cover and refrigerate until cold.

6 Taste and adjust the seasoning. For a more spicy soup, stir in a little chilli purée to taste. For a thinner soup, add a small amount of iced water. Ladle into chilled bowls and garnish with finely chopped red pepper and/or chillies.

Thai Fish Soup

This is also known as Tom Yam Gung. Asian supermarkets may sell tom yam sauce ready prepared in jars, sometimes labelled 'Chillies in Oil'.

NUTRITIONAL INFORMATION

Calories ....230 Sugars 4g
Protein ....22g Fat 12g
Carbohydrate ....9g Saturates 1g

25 mins   20 mins

SERVES 4

INGREDIENTS

450 ml/16 fl oz light chicken stock

2 lime leaves, chopped

5–cm/2–inch piece lemon grass, chopped

3 tbsp lemon juice

3 tbsp Thai fish sauce

2 small, hot green chillies, deseeded and finely chopped

½ tsp sugar

8 small shiitake mushrooms or 8 straw mushrooms, halved

450 g/1 lb raw prawns, peeled if necessary and de-veined

spring onions, to garnish

TOM YAM SAUCE

4 tbsp vegetable oil

5 garlic cloves, finely chopped

1 large shallot, finely chopped

2 large hot dried red chillies, roughly chopped

1 tbsp dried shrimp (optional)

1 tbsp Thai fish sauce

2 tsp sugar

1 First make the tom yam sauce. Heat the oil in a small frying pan and add the garlic. Cook for a few seconds until the garlic just browns. Remove with a slotted spoon and set aside. Add the shallot to the same oil and fry until browned and crisp. Remove with a slotted spoon and set aside. Add the chillies and fry until they darken. Remove from the oil and drain on kitchen paper. Remove the frying pan from the hob, reserve the oil.

2 In a small food processor or spice grinder, grind the dried shrimp, if using, then add the reserved chillies, garlic and shallots. Grind together to a smooth paste. Return the pan with the original oil to a low heat, add the paste and warm. Add the fish sauce and sugar and mix. Remove from the heat.

3 In a large saucepan, heat together the stock and 2 tablespoons of the tom yam sauce. Add the lime leaves, lemon grass, lemon juice, fish sauce, chillies and sugar. Simmer for 2 minutes.

4 Add the mushrooms and prawns and cook a further 2–3 minutes until the prawns are cooked. Ladle in to warm bowls and serve immediately, garnished with spring onion.

Sweetcorn & Crab Soup

This speedy soup is a good standby, made in a matter of minutes.
If you prefer, you can use frozen crab sticks.

NUTRITIONAL INFORMATION

Calories 183	Sugars 9g
Protein 7g	Fat 6g
Carbohydrate ...26g	Saturates 1g

 5–10 mins   15–20 mins

SERVES 4

I N G R E D I E N T S

1 tbsp vegetable oil

3 garlic cloves, crushed

1 tsp fresh ginger root, grated

700 ml/1¼ pints chicken stock

375 g/13 oz canned creamed sweetcorn

1 tbsp Thai fish sauce

175 g/6 oz canned white crabmeat, drained

1 egg

salt and pepper

fresh coriander, shredded, and paprika,
   to garnish

1 Heat the vegetable oil in a large saucepan and fry the garlic for 1 minute, stirring constantly.

2 Add the ginger then stir in the stock and sweetcorn. Bring to the boil.

3 Stir in the fish sauce, crabmeat and salt and pepper. Return to the boil.

4 Beat the egg, then stir lightly into the soup so that it sets into long strands. Simmer gently for about 30 seconds until the egg is just set.

5 Ladle the soup into bowls and serve it piping hot, garnished with fresh shredded coriander leaves and paprika sprinkled over the surface.

COOK'S TIP

To give the soup an extra rich flavour kick for a special occasion, stir in 1 tablespoon of dry sherry or rice wine just before you ladle it into warm soup bowls.

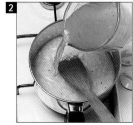

Pumpkin & Coconut Soup

This substantial soup is filling and, if served with crusty bread, is all you need for a satisfying lunch.

NUTRITIONAL INFORMATION

Calories 105   Sugars 6g
Protein . . . . .3g   Fat 7g
Carbohydrate . . . .8g   Saturates 4g

 20 mins   45–50 mins

SERVES 6

INGREDIENTS

1 kg/2 lb 4 oz pumpkin

1 tbsp groundnut oil

1 tsp yellow mustard seeds

1 garlic clove, crushed

1 large onion, chopped

1 celery stick, chopped

1 small red chilli, chopped

850 ml/1½ pints stock

1 tbsp dried prawns

5 tbsp coconut cream

salt and pepper

extra coconut cream, to garnish

1 Halve the pumpkin and remove the seeds. Cut away the skin and dice the pumpkin flesh.

2 Heat the oil in a large flameproof casserole and fry the mustard seeds until they begin to pop. Stir in the garlic, onion, celery and chilli, and stir-fry for 1–2 minutes.

3 Add the pumpkin with the stock and dried prawns and bring to the boil. Lower the heat, cover and simmer gently for about 30 minutes until the ingredients are very tender.

4 Transfer the mixture to a food processor or a blender, and process until smooth. Return the mixture to the pan and stir in the coconut cream.

5 Adjust the seasoning to taste with salt and pepper and serve hot, with coconut cream swirled in each bowl. For an extra touch of garnish, swirl a spoonful of thick coconut milk into each bowl of soup as you serve it.

Mushroom & Tofu Broth

Dried black mushrooms are sold in Asian stores, and although they can be expensive, they are worth searching out.

NUTRITIONAL INFORMATION

Calories	65	Sugars	.....1g
Protein	.....4g	Fat	.....5g
Carbohydrate	.....2g	Saturates	.....1g

 10 mins, plus soaking time   10–15 mins

SERVES 4

INGREDIENTS

4 dried black mushrooms

1 tbsp sunflower oil

1 tsp sesame oil

1 garlic clove, crushed

1 green chilli, deseeded and finely chopped

6 spring onions

1 litre/1¾ pints rich brown stock

85 g/3 oz fresh oyster mushrooms, sliced

2 kaffir lime leaves, finely shredded

2 tbsp lime juice

1 tbsp rice vinegar

1 tbsp Thai fish sauce

85 g/3 oz firm tofu, diced

salt and pepper

COOK'S TIP

Stock cubes make a cloudy broth, so use a clear, richly coloured, home-made beef stock, or a Japanese dashi. For a vegetarian broth, use a well-flavoured vegetable stock and light soy sauce.

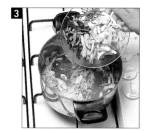

1 Pour 150 ml/5 fl oz boiling water over the dried black mushrooms and leave to soak for about 30 minutes. Drain, reserving the liquid, then chop the black mushrooms roughly.

2 Heat the sunflower and sesame oils in a large pan or wok over a high heat. Add the garlic, chilli and spring onions, and stir the mixture for 1 minute until it is softened but not browned.

3 Add the mushrooms, lime leaves, stock, and reserved mushroom liquid, and bring to the boil.

4 Stir in the lime juice, rice vinegar and fish sauce, lower the heat and simmer gently for 3–4 minutes.

5 Add the tofu and season to taste. Heat gently until boiling, and serve.

Rice Soup with Eggs

This version of a classic Thai soup, sometimes eaten for breakfast, is a good way of using up any leftover cooked rice.

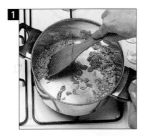

NUTRITIONAL INFORMATION

Calories	197	Sugars	.........1g
Protein	........11g	Fat	..........10g
Carbohydrate	...17g	Saturates	.......2g

 10 mins   20 mins

SERVES 4

I N G R E D I E N T S

1 tsp sunflower oil

1 garlic clove, crushed

50 g/1¾ oz minced pork

3 spring onions, sliced

1 tbsp fresh ginger root, grated

1 red bird-eye chilli, deseeded and chopped

1 litre/1¾ pints chicken stock

200 g/7 oz cooked long-grain rice

1 tbsp Thai fish sauce

4 small eggs

salt and pepper

2 tbsp fresh coriander, shredded, to garnish

1 Heat the oil in a large pan or wok. Add the garlic and pork and fry gently for about 1 minute until the meat is broken up but not browned.

2 Stir in the spring onions, ginger, chilli and stock, stirring until boiling. Add the rice, lower the heat and simmer for 2 minutes.

3 Add the fish sauce and adjust the seasoning with salt and pepper to taste. Carefully break the eggs into the soup and simmer over a very low heat for 3–4 minutes until set.

4 Ladle the soup into large bowls, allowing 1 egg per portion. Garnish with shredded coriander leaves and serve immediately.

COOK'S TIP
If you prefer, beat the eggs together and fry them like an omelette until set, then cut into ribbon-like strips and add to the soup just before serving.

Spinach & Ginger Soup

This mildly spiced, rich green soup is delicately scented with ginger and lemon grass. It makes a good light starter or summer lunch.

NUTRITIONAL INFORMATION

Calories	38	Sugars	. . . . . . .0.8g
Protein	. . . . .3.2g	Fat	. . . . .1.8g
Carbohydrate	. . .2.4g	Saturates	. . . . .0.2g

 10 mins   25 mins

SERVES 4

INGREDIENTS

2 tbsp sunflower oil

1 onion, chopped

2 garlic cloves, finely chopped

2.5 cm/1 inch piece ginger root, finely chopped

250 g/9 oz fresh young spinach leaves

1 small lemon grass stalk, finely chopped

1 litre/1¾ pints chicken or vegetable stock

1 small potato, peeled and chopped

1 tbsp rice wine or dry sherry

1 tsp sesame oil

salt and pepper

fresh spinach, finely shredded, to garnish

1 Heat the oil in a large saucepan. Add the onion, garlic and ginger, and fry gently for 3–4 minutes until softened.

2 Reserve 2–3 small spinach leaves. Add the remaining leaves and lemon grass to the saucepan, stirring until the spinach is wilted. Add the stock and potato to the pan and bring to the boil. Lower the heat, cover and simmer for about 10 minutes.

3 Tip the soup into a blender or food processor and process until completely smooth.

4 Return the soup to the pan and add the rice wine, then adjust the seasoning to taste with salt and pepper. Heat until just about to boil.

5 Finely shred the reserved spinach leaves and scatter some over the top. Drizzle with a few drops of sesame oil and serve hot, garnished with the finely shredded fresh spinach leaves.

VARIATION

To make a creamy spinach and coconut soup, stir in 4 tablespoons creamed coconut, or replace 300 ml/ 10 fl oz of stock with coconut milk. Scatter fresh coconut shavings over the soup.

Chilled Avocado Soup

A delightfully simple soup with a blend of typical Thai flavours, which needs no cooking and can be served at any time of day.

NUTRITIONAL INFORMATION

Calories ....188 Sugars 2g
Protein ....3g Fat 18g
Carbohydrate ....4g Saturates 5g

10-15 mins   0 mins

SERVES 4

INGREDIENTS

2 ripe avocados

1 small mild onion, chopped

1 garlic clove, crushed

2 tbsp fresh coriander, chopped

1 tbsp fresh mint, chopped

2 tbsp lime juice

700 ml/1¼ pints vegetable stock

1 tbsp rice vinegar

1 tbsp light soy sauce

salt and pepper

GARNISH

2 tbsp soured cream or crème fraîche

1 tbsp fresh coriander,
   finely chopped

2 tsp lime juice

lime rind, finely shredded

1 Halve, stone and scoop out the flesh from the avocados. Place in a blender or food processor with the onion, garlic, coriander, mint, lime juice and about half the stock, and process until completely smooth.

2 Add the remaining stock, rice vinegar and soy sauce and blend again to mix well. Taste and adjust seasoning if necessary with salt and pepper, or with a little extra lime juice if required. Cover the soup and chill in the refrigerator until it is needed.

3 To make the lime and coriander cream garnish, mix together the soured cream, coriander and lime juice. Spoon into the soup just before serving and sprinkle with lime rind.

COOK'S TIP

The surface of the soup may darken if the soup is stored for longer than an hour. Give it a quick stir before serving. If you plan to keep the soup for several hours, lay cling film over the surface to seal it.

Prawn Satay

It is well worth seeking a supplier of Thai ingredients, such as lemon grass and lime leaves, as they add such distinctive flavours.

NUTRITIONAL INFORMATION

Calories	367	Sugars	........25g
Protein	.........9g	Fat	..........23g
Carbohydrate	...33g	Saturates	.......3g

  15 mins   15–20 mins

SERVES 4

INGREDIENTS

12 peeled raw king prawns

MARINADE

1 tsp ground coriander

1 tsp ground cumin

2 tbsp light soy sauce

4 tbsp vegetable oil

1 tbsp curry powder

1 tbsp ground turmeric

125 ml/4 fl oz coconut milk

3 tbsp sugar

PEANUT SAUCE

2 tbsp vegetable oil

3 garlic cloves, crushed

1 tbsp red curry paste (see Red Prawn Curry, page 47)

125 ml/4 fl oz coconut milk

225 ml/8 fl oz fish or chicken stock

1 tbsp sugar

1 tsp salt

1 tbsp lemon juice

4 tbsp unsalted roasted peanuts, finely chopped

4 tbsp dried breadcrumbs

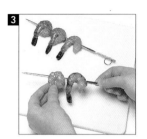

1 Slit the prawns down their backs and remove the black vein, if any. Set aside. Mix together the marinade ingredients and add the prawns. Mix together well, cover and set aside for at least 8 hours or overnight.

2 To make the peanut sauce, heat the oil in a large frying pan until very hot. Add the garlic and fry until just starting to colour. Add the curry paste and mix together well, cooking for a further 30 seconds. Add the coconut milk, stock, sugar, salt and lemon juice and stir well. Boil for 1–2 minutes, stirring constantly. Add the peanuts and breadcrumbs and mix together well. Pour the sauce into a bowl and set aside.

3 Using 4 skewers, thread 3 prawns on to each. Cook under a preheated hot grill or on the barbecue for about 3–4 minutes on each side until just cooked through. Serve immediately with the peanut sauce.

Sweet & Sour Fish Cakes

If you can find them, use small chillies, called bird-eye, for the dipping sauce. They are very hot however, so remove the seeds if you prefer.

NUTRITIONAL INFORMATION

Calories 213	Sugars 23g	
Protein 21g	Fat 4g	
Carbohydrate . . .25g	Saturates 1g	

15 mins   10 mins

SERVES 4

INGREDIENTS

450 g/1 lb firm white fish, such as hake, haddock or cod, skinned and roughly chopped

1 tbsp Thai fish sauce

1 tbsp red curry paste (see Red Prawn Curry, page 47)

1 kaffir lime leaf, finely shredded

2 tbsp chopped fresh coriander

1 egg

1 tsp brown sugar

large pinch salt

40 g/1½ oz green beans, thinly sliced crossways

vegetable oil, for shallow-frying

SWEET-AND-SOUR DIPPING SAUCE

4 tbsp sugar

1 tbsp cold water

3 tbsp white rice vinegar

2 small, hot chillies, finely chopped

1 tbsp fish sauce

1 For the fish cakes, put the fish, fish sauce, curry paste, lime leaf, coriander, egg, sugar and salt into the bowl of a food processor. Process until smooth. Scrape into a bowl and stir in the green beans. Set aside.

2 To make the sauce, put the sugar, water and rice vinegar into a saucepan and heat gently until the sugar has dissolved. Bring to the boil and simmer for 2 minutes. Remove from the heat, stir in the chillies and fish sauce and leave to cool.

3 Heat a frying pan with enough oil to generously cover the bottom. Divide the fish mixture into 16 little balls. Flatten the balls into little patties and fry in the hot oil for 1-2 minutes each side until golden. Drain on paper towels. Serve hot with the dipping sauce.

COOK'S TIP

It isn't necessary to use the most expensive cut of white fish in this recipe as the other flavours are very strong. Use whatever is cheapest.

Thai Noodles

This is a delicious classic Thai noodle dish, flavoured with fish sauce, roasted peanuts and prawns.

NUTRITIONAL INFORMATION

Calories	344	Sugars	.........2g
Protein	........21g	Fat	..........17g
Carbohydrate	...27g	Saturates	.......2g

 20 mins   10–15 mins

SERVES 4

INGREDIENTS

350 g/12 oz cooked, peeled tiger prawns

115 g/4 oz flat rice noodles or
  rice vermicelli

4 tbsp vegetable oil

2 garlic cloves, finely chopped

1 egg

2 tbsp lemon juice

1½ tbsp Thai fish sauce

½ tsp sugar

2 tbsp chopped, roasted peanuts

½ tsp cayenne pepper

2 spring onions, cut into
  2.5 cm/1 inch pieces

50 g/1¾ oz fresh beansprouts

1 tbsp chopped fresh coriander

lemon wedges, to serve

1 Drain the prawns on kitchen paper to remove excess moisture. Cook the noodles. Drain well and set aside.

2 Heat the oil in a frying pan. Fry the garlic until golden. Add the egg and stir to break it up. Cook for a few seconds.

3 Add the prawns and noodles and mix thoroughly with the egg and garlic.

4 Add the lemon juice, fish sauce, sugar, half the peanuts, cayenne pepper, spring onions and half the beansprouts stirring quickly all the time. Cook over a high heat for a further 2 minutes.

5 Turn on to a serving plate. Top with the remaining peanuts and bean-sprouts and sprinkle with the coriander. Serve with lemon wedges.

VARIATION

This is a basic dish to which lots of different cooked seafood could be added. Cooked squid rings, mussels and langoustines would all work just as well as the prawns.

Fish Cakes with Hot Sauce

These little fish cakes are very popular in Thailand as street food and make a perfect snack. Also, serve them as a starter.

NUTRITIONAL INFORMATION

Calories 205	Sugars 6g
Protein 17g	Fat 12g
Carbohydrate 7g	Saturates 2g

10 mins   10–20 m0ins

SERVES 4–5

INGREDIENTS

350 g/12 oz white fish fillet without skin, such as cod or haddock

1 tbsp Thai fish sauce

2 tsp Thai red curry paste

1 tbsp lime juice

1 garlic clove, crushed

4 dried kaffir lime leaves, crumbled

1 egg white

3 tbsp fresh coriander, chopped

salt and pepper

vegetable oil for shallow frying

green salad leaves, to serve

PEANUT DIP

1 small red chilli

1 tbsp light soy sauce

1 tbsp lime juice

1 tbsp soft light brown sugar

3 tbsp chunky peanut butter

4 tbsp coconut milk

1 Put the fish fillet in a food processor with the fish sauce, curry paste, lime juice, garlic, lime leaves and egg white, and process until a smooth paste forms.

2 Stir in the fresh coriander and quickly process again until mixed. Divide the mixture into 8–10 pieces and roll into balls, then flatten to make round patties and set aside.

3 For the dip, deseed the chilli and chop it finely. Place in a pan with the remaining ingredients and heat gently, stirring constantly to blend. Adjust the seasoning.

4 Shallow fry the fish cakes for 3–4 minutes on each side until golden brown. Drain on kitchen paper and serve hot on a bed of green salad with the dip.

Thai-style Crab Sandwich

A hearty, open sandwich, topped with a classic flavour combination – crab with avocado and ginger. Perfect for a light summer lunch.

NUTRITIONAL INFORMATION

Calories	768	Sugars	.........3g
Protein	........26g	Fat	..........49g
Carbohydrate	...58g	Saturates	.......8g

 5–10 mins   0 mins

SERVES 2

INGREDIENTS

2 tbsp lime juice

2 cm/¾ inch piece fresh ginger root, grated

2 cm/¾ inch piece lemon grass, finely chopped

5 tbsp mayonnaise

2 large slices crusty bread

1 ripe avocado

150 g/5½ oz cooked crab meat

black pepper, freshly ground

sprigs fresh coriander, to garnish

1 Mix half the lime juice with the ginger and lemon grass. Add the mayonnaise and mix well.

2 Spread 1 tablespoon of mayonnaise smoothly over each slice of bread.

3 Halve the avocado and remove the stone. Peel and slice the flesh thinly, then arrange the avocado slices on the slices of bread. Sprinkle lime juice over the avocado.

4 Spoon the cooked crab meat over the avocado slices, then add any of the remaining lime juice. Spoon the remaining mayonnaise over the sandwiches, season to taste with freshly ground black pepper, top with a fresh coriander sprig and serve immediately.

COOK'S TIP

To make lime-and-ginger mayonnaise, place 2 egg yolks, 1 tablespoon lime juice and ½ teaspoon grated ginger root in a blender. With the motor running, add 300 ml/10 fl oz olive oil, drop by drop, until thick and smooth. Season with salt and pepper and serve.

Sticky Ginger Chicken Wings

A finger-licking starter that's ideal for parties – but have some finger bowls ready. If you can't get chicken wings for this recipe, use drumsticks instead.

NUTRITIONAL INFORMATION

Calories	416	Sugars	.........5g
Protein	........41g	Fat	..........25g
Carbohydrate	....7g	Saturates	.......7g

 30 mins   12–15 mins

SERVES 4

INGREDIENTS

2 garlic cloves, peeled

1 piece stem ginger in syrup

1 tsp coriander seeds

2 tbsp dark soy sauce

1 tbsp lime juice

1 tsp sesame oil

12 chicken wings

lime wedges and fresh coriander leaves, to garnish

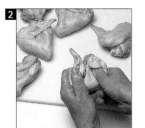

1 Roughly chop the garlic and stem ginger. In a pestle and mortar, crush the garlic, stem ginger and coriander seeds to a paste, gradually working in the ginger syrup, soy sauce, lime juice and sesame oil.

2 Tuck the pointed tip of each chicken wing underneath the thicker end of the wing to make a neat triangular shape. Place in a large bowl.

3 Add the garlic and ginger paste to the bowl and toss the chicken wings in the mixture to coat evenly. Cover and leave in the refrigerator to marinate for several hours or overnight.

4 Arrange the chicken wings in one layer on a foil-lined grill pan and cook under a medium-hot grill for 12–15 minutes, turning them occasionally, until they are golden brown and thoroughly cooked through.

5 Alternatively, cook on a lightly oiled barbecue grill over medium-hot coals for 12–15 minutes. To serve, garnish with lime wedges and fresh coriander.

COOK'S TIP
To test if the chicken is cooked, pierce it deeply through the thickest part of the flesh. It is cooked when the chicken juices are clear, with no trace of pink.

Lemon Grass Chicken

An unusual recipe in which fresh lemon grass stalks are used as skewers, which impart their delicate lemon flavour to the chicken mixture.

NUTRITIONAL INFORMATION

Calories 140	Sugars 2g	
Protein 19g	Fat 7g	
Carbohydrate 2g	Saturates 1g	

25 mins · 4–6 mins

SERVES 4

INGREDIENTS

2 long or 4 short lemon grass stalks

2 large boneless, skinless chicken breasts (halves), about 400 g/14 oz in total

1 small egg white

1 carrot, finely grated

1 small red chilli, deseeded and chopped

2 tbsp fresh garlic chives, chopped

2 tbsp fresh coriander, chopped

1 tbsp sunflower oil

salt and pepper

fresh coriander and lime slices, to garnish

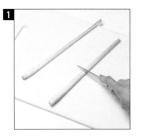

1 If the lemon grass stalks are long, cut them in half across the middle to make 4 short lengths. Cut each stalk in half lengthways, so that you have 8 sticks.

COOK'S TIP

If you can't find whole lemon grass stalks, use wooden or bamboo skewers instead, and add ½ teaspoon ground lemon grass to the mixture with the other flavourings.

2 Roughly chop the chicken and place in a food processor with the egg white. Process to a smooth paste, then add the carrot, chilli, chives, coriander, salt and pepper. Process for a few seconds to mix.

3 Chill the mixture in the refrigerator for about 15 minutes. Divide the mixture into 8 equal portions, and use your hands to shape the mixture around the lemon grass 'skewers'.

4 Brush the skewers with oil and grill under a preheated medium-hot grill for 4–6 minutes, turning them occasionally, until golden brown and thoroughly cooked. Alternatively, barbecue the skewers over medium-hot coals.

5 Serve hot, and garnish with fresh coriander and slices of lime.

Thai Stuffed Omelette

This omelette may be a substantial starter or a light dish for lunch or supper. Serve it accompanied by a colourful, crisp salad.

NUTRITIONAL INFORMATION

Calories 270	Sugars 1g	
Protein 24g	Fat 18g	
Carbohydrate 2g	Saturates 4g	

 10 mins   30-40 mins

SERVES 4

I N G R E D I E N T S

2 garlic cloves, chopped

4 black peppercorns

4 sprigs fresh coriander

2 tbsp vegetable oil

200 g/7 oz minced pork

2 spring onions, chopped

1 large, firm tomato, chopped

6 large eggs

1 tbsp Thai fish sauce

¼ tsp turmeric

mixed salad leaves, tossed, to serve

1 Place the garlic, peppercorns and coriander in a pestle and mortar and crush until a smooth paste forms.

2 Heat 1 tablespoon of oil in a wok over a medium heat. Add the paste and fry for 1–2 minutes until it just turns colour.

3 Stir in the pork and stir-fry until it is lightly browned. Add the spring onions and tomato, stir-fry for a further minute, then remove from the heat.

4 Heat the remaining oil in a frying pan. Beat the eggs with the fish sauce and turmeric, then pour a quarter of the egg mixture into the pan. As the mixture begins to set, stir it very lightly to ensure that all the liquid egg is set.

5 Spoon a quarter of the pork mixture down the centre of the omelette, then fold the sides inwards towards the centre, enclosing the filling. Make 3 more omelettes.

6 Slide the omelettes on to a serving plate and serve with a mixed salad.

COOK'S TIP

If you prefer, spread half the pork mixture evenly over one omelette, then place a second omelette on top, without folding. Cut into slim wedges to serve.

Thai-spiced Sausages

These mildly spiced little sausages are ideal for a buffet meal. They can be made a day in advance, and are equally good served hot or cold.

NUTRITIONAL INFORMATION

Calories	206	Sugars	.......0.1g
Protein	........22g	Fat	...........11g
Carbohydrate	....4g	Saturates	.......2g

20-25 mins   8-10 mins

SERVES 4

INGREDIENTS

400 g/14 oz lean minced pork

4 tbsp cooked rice

1 garlic clove, crushed

1 tsp Thai red curry paste

1 tsp ground black pepper

1 tsp ground coriander

½ tsp salt

3 tbsp lime juice

2 tbsp fresh coriander, chopped

3 tbsp groundnut oil

coconut sambal or soy sauce, to serve

1 Place the pork, rice, garlic, curry paste, pepper, ground coriander, salt, lime juice and fresh coriander in a bowl and knead together with your hands to mix evenly.

2 Shape the mixture into 12 small sausage shapes. If you can buy sausage casings, fill the casings and twist at intervals to separate the sausages.

3 Heat the oil in a large frying pan over a medium heat. Add the sausages – in batches if necessary, and fry for 8–10 minutes, turning them over occasionally, until they are evenly golden brown. Serve hot with a coconut sambal or soy sauce.

COOK'S TIP

These sausages can also be served as a starter – shape the mixture slightly smaller to make about 16 bite-sized sausages. Serve with a soy dip.

Thai-style Burgers

If your family likes to eat burgers, try these – they have a much more interesting flavour than conventional hamburgers.

NUTRITIONAL INFORMATION

Calories	358	Sugars	.........1g
Protein	........23g	Fat	..........29g
Carbohydrate	....2g	Saturates	.......5g

🧊 20 mins   🕐 6–8 mins

SERVES 4

INGREDIENTS

1 small lemon grass stalk

1 small red chilli, deseeded

2 garlic cloves, peeled

2 spring onions

200 g/7 oz closed-cup mushrooms

400 g/14 oz minced pork

1 tbsp Thai fish sauce

3 tbsp fresh coriander, chopped

sunflower oil for shallow frying

2 tbsp mayonnaise

1 tbsp lime juice

salt and pepper

TO SERVE

4 sesame hamburger buns

shredded Chinese leaves

1 Place the lemon grass, chilli, garlic and spring onions in a food processor and process to a smooth paste. Add the mushrooms and process until they are very finely chopped.

2 Add the minced pork, fish sauce and coriander. Season well with salt and pepper, then divide the mixture into 4 equal portions and shape with lightly floured hands into flat burger shapes.

3 Heat the oil in a frying pan over a medium heat. Add the burgers and fry for 6–8 minutes until done or as you like.

4 Meanwhile, mix the mayonnaise with the lime juice. Split the hamburger buns and spread the lime-flavoured mayonnaise on the cut surfaces. Add a few shredded Chinese leaves, top with a burger and sandwich together. Serve immediately, while still hot.

COOK'S TIP

You can add a spoonful of your favourite relish to each burger, or alternatively, add a few pieces of crisp pickled vegetables for a change of texture.

Hot & Sour Noodles

This simple, fast-food dish is sold from street food stalls in Thailand, with many and varied additions of meat and vegetables.

NUTRITIONAL INFORMATION

Calories	337	Sugars	.........1g
Protein	........10g	Fat	...........11g
Carbohydrate	...53g	Saturates	.......1g

 10 mins   10–15 mins

SERVES 4

I N G R E D I E N T S

250 g/9 oz dried medium egg noodles

1 tbsp sesame oil

1 tbsp chilli oil

1 garlic clove, crushed

2 spring onions, finely chopped

55 g/2 oz/⅔ cup button mushrooms, sliced

40 g/1½ oz dried Chinese black mushrooms, soaked, drained and sliced

2 tbsp lime juice

3 tbsp light soy sauce

1 tsp sugar

TO SERVE

shredded Chinese leaves

2 tbsp shredded coriander

2 tbsp toasted peanuts, chopped

COOK'S TIP

Thai chilli oil is very hot, so if you want a milder flavour, use vegetable oil for the initial cooking instead, then add a final dribble of chilli oil just for seasoning.

1 Cook the egg noodles in a large saucepan of boiling water for about 3–4 minutes, or according to the packet directions. Drain well, return to the pan, then toss the noodles with the sesame oil and set aside.

2 Heat the chilli oil in a large frying pan or wok and quickly stir-fry the garlic, spring onions and button mushrooms to soften them.

3 Add the black mushrooms, lime juice, soy sauce and sugar and continue stir-frying until boiling. Add the noodles and toss to mix.

4 Serve the hot-and-sour noodles spooned over shredded Chinese leaves, sprinkled with coriander and peanuts.

Pad Thai Noodles

The combination of ingredients in this classic dish varies, depending on the cook, but it commonly contains a mixture of pork and prawns

NUTRITIONAL INFORMATION

Calories 477	Sugars 6g	
Protein 26g	Fat 14g	
Carbohydrate ...60g	Saturates 3g	

 15 mins   10–15 mins

SERVES 4

I N G R E D I E N T S

250 g/9 oz rice stick noodles

3 tbsp groundnut oil

3 garlic cloves, finely chopped

125 g/4½ oz pork fillet, chopped into 5 mm/
¼ inch pieces

200 g/7 oz prawns, peeled

1 tbsp sugar

3 tbsp Thai fish sauce

1 tbsp tomato ketchup

1 tbsp lime juice

2 eggs, beaten

125 g/4½ oz beansprouts

TO GARNISH

1 tsp dried red chilli flakes

2 spring onions, thickly sliced

2 tbsp fresh coriander, chopped

1 Soak the rice noodles in hot water for about 15 minutes, or according to the packet directions. Drain the cooked noodles well and put them to one side.

2 Heat the oil in a large frying pan or wok and fry the garlic over a high heat for 30 seconds. Add the pork and stir-fry evenly for 2–3 minutes until the meat is browned.

3 Stir in the prawns, add the sugar, fish sauce, ketchup and lime juice and continue stir-fry for another 30 seconds.

4 Stir in the eggs and stir-fry until lightly set. Stir in the noodles, then add the beansprouts and stir-fry for a further 30 seconds to cook lightly.

5 Transfer to a plate. Scatter with chilli flakes, spring onions and coriander.

COOK'S TIP
Drain the rice noodles thoroughly before adding to the pan, as excess moisture will spoil the texture of the dish.

Rice Noodles & Mushrooms

An alternative to classic noodle dishes such as Pad Thai Noodles, this quick and easy dish contains tofu and is very filling.

NUTRITIONAL INFORMATION

Calories	361	Sugars	. . . . .3g
Protein	. . . . .9g	Fat	. . . . .12g
Carbohydrate	. . .53g	Saturates	. . . . . . .2g

 15 mins   10 mins

SERVES 4

INGREDIENTS

225 g/8 oz rice stick noodles

2 tbsp vegetable oil

1 garlic clove, finely chopped

2 cm/¾ inch piece fresh ginger root,
 finely chopped

4 shallots, thinly sliced

70 g/2½ oz shiitake mushrooms, sliced

100 g/3½ oz firm tofu, cut into
 1.5 cm/⅝ inch dice

2 tbsp light soy sauce

1 tbsp rice wine

1 tbsp Thai fish sauce

1 tbsp smooth peanut butter

1 tsp chilli sauce

2 tbsp toasted peanuts, chopped

shredded basil leaves, to serve

1 Soak the rice stick noodles in hot water for 15 minutes, or according to the packet directions. Drain well.

2 Heat the oil in a frying pan and stir-fry the garlic, ginger and shallots for 1–2 minutes until softened and lightly browned.

3 Add the mushrooms to the pan and stir-fry for a further 2–3 minutes. Stir in the tofu and toss gently to brown lightly.

4 Mix together the soy sauce, rice wine, fish sauce, peanut butter and chilli sauce, then stir into the pan.

5 Stir in the rice noodles and toss to coat evenly in the sauce. Scatter with the chopped peanuts and shredded basil leaves and serve hot.

COOK'S TIP

Replace the shiitake mushrooms with a can of Chinese straw mushrooms. Alternatively, use dried shiitake mushrooms, soaked and drained before use.

Drunken Noodles

Perhaps this would be more correctly named 'drunkards' noodles', as it's supposedly often eaten as a hangover cure.

NUTRITIONAL INFORMATION

Calories	278	Sugars	.........3g
Protein	........12g	Fat	...........7g
Carbohydrate	...40g	Saturates	.......1g

 15 mins   10 mins

SERVES 4

INGREDIENTS

175 g/6 oz rice stick noodles

2 tbsp vegetable oil

1 garlic clove, crushed

2 small green chillies, chopped

1 small onion, thinly sliced

150 g/5½ oz lean minced pork
  or chicken

1 small green pepper, deseeded and
  finely chopped

4 kaffir lime leaves, finely shredded

1 tbsp dark soy sauce

1 tbsp light soy sauce

½ tsp sugar

1 tomato, cut into thin wedges

2 tbsp sweet basil leaves, finely sliced,
  to garnish

1 Soak the rice stick noodles in hot water for 15 minutes, or according to the packet directions. Drain well.

2 Heat the oil in a wok and stir-fry the garlic, chillies and onion for 1 minute.

3 Stir in the pork or chicken and stir-fry on a high heat for a further minute, then add the pepper and continue stir-frying for a further 2 minutes.

4 Stir in the lime leaves, soy sauces and sugar. Add the noodles and tomato and toss well to heat thoroughly.

5 Sprinkle the drunken noodles with the sliced basil leaves and serve hot.

COOK'S TIP

Fresh kaffir lime leaves freeze well. Simply tie them in a tightly sealed polythene freezer bag and freeze for up to a month. They can be used straight from the freezer.

Rice Noodles with Chicken

The great thing about stir-fries is you can use very little fat and still get lots of flavour, as in this light, healthy lunch dish that is low in fat.

NUTRITIONAL INFORMATION

Calories 329   Sugars 3g
Protein . . . . .25g   Fat 4g
Carbohydrate . . .46g   Saturates 1g

 15 mins   10 mins

SERVES 4

I N G R E D I E N T S

200 g/7 oz rice stick noodles

1 tbsp sunflower oil

1 garlic clove, finely chopped

2 cm/¾ inch piece fresh ginger root, finely chopped

4 spring onions, chopped

1 red bird-eye chilli, deseeded and sliced

300 g/10½ oz boneless, skinless chicken, finely chopped

2 chicken livers, finely chopped

1 celery stick, thinly sliced

1 carrot, cut into fine matchsticks

300 g/10½ oz shredded Chinese leaves

4 tbsp lime juice

2 tbsp Thai fish sauce

1 tbsp soy sauce

TO GARNISH

2 tbsp fresh mint, shredded

slices of pickled garlic

fresh mint sprig

1 Soak the rice noodles in hot water for 15 minutes, or according to the package directions. Drain well.

2 Heat the oil in a wok or large frying pan and stir-fry the garlic, ginger, spring onions and chilli for about 1 minute. Stir in the chicken and chicken livers, then stir-fry over a high heat for 2–3 minutes until beginning to brown.

3 Stir in the celery and carrot and stir-fry for 2 minutes to soften. Add the Chinese leaves, then stir in the lime juice, fish sauce and soy sauce.

4 Add the noodles and stir to heat thoroughly. Sprinkle with shredded mint and pickled garlic. Serve immediately, garnished with a mint sprig.

Stir-fried Pork with Pasta

This delicious dish, with its flavourful hint of Thai cuisine, will certainly get the tastebuds tingling.

NUTRITIONAL INFORMATION

Calories 751   Sugars 10g
Protein . . . . .37g   Fat 27g
Carbohydrate . . .96g   Saturates 8g

 20 mins   15 mins

SERVES 4

INGREDIENTS

3 tbsp sesame oil

350 g/12 oz pork fillet, cut into thin strips

450 g/1 lb dried taglioni

1 tbsp olive oil

8 shallots, sliced

2 garlic cloves, finely chopped

2.5 cm/1 inch piece fresh ginger root, grated

1 fresh green chilli, finely chopped

1 red pepper, cored, seeded and thinly sliced

1 green pepper, cored, seeded and thinly sliced

3 courgettes, thinly sliced

2 tbsp ground almonds

1 tsp ground cinnamon

1 tbsp oyster sauce

55 g/2 oz creamed coconut (see Cook's Tip, below), grated

salt and pepper

1 Heat the oil in a wok. Season the pork and stir-fry for 5 minutes.

2 Bring a saucepan of lightly salted water to the boil. Add the taglioni and olive oil and cook for about 12 minutes, until just tender, but still firm to the bite. Set aside and keep warm until required.

3 Add the shallots, garlic, ginger and chilli to the wok and stir-fry for 2 minutes. Add the peppers and courgettes and stir-fry for 1 minute.

4 Add the ground almonds, cinnamon, oyster sauce and creamed coconut to the wok and stir-fry for 1 minute.

5 Drain the taglioni and transfer to a dish. Top with the stir-fry and serve.

COOK'S TIP
Creamed coconut is available from Chinese and Asian food stores and some large supermarkets. It is sold in the form of compressed blocks and adds a concentrated coconut flavour to the dish.

Pad Thai Noodles

All over Thailand and South East Asia, cooks sell these simple delicious rice noodles, stir-fried to order, from streetside stalls and from boats.

NUTRITIONAL INFORMATION

Calories 527   Sugars 8g
Protein . . . . .34g   Fat 17g
Carbohydrate . . .58g   Saturates 3g

 15 mins   10 mins

SERVES 4

I N G R E D I E N T S

225 g/8 oz flat rice noodles (sen lek)

2 tbsp groundnut or vegetable oil

225 g/8 oz boneless chicken breasts, skinned and thinly sliced

4 shallots, finely chopped

2 garlic cloves, finely chopped

4 spring onions, cut on the diagonal into 5 cm/2 inch pieces

350 g/12 oz fresh white crab meat

75 g/2¾ oz fresh beansprouts, rinsed

1 tbsp preserved radish or fresh radish, finely diced

2–4 tbsp roasted peanuts, chopped

fresh coriander sprigs, to garnish

S A U C E

3 tbsp Thai fish sauce

2–3 tbsp rice vinegar or cider vinegar

1 tbsp chilli bean sauce or oyster sauce

1 tbsp toasted sesame oil

1 tbsp palm sugar or light brown sugar

½ tsp cayenne pepper or fresh red chilli, thinly sliced

1 To make the sauce, whisk together the sauce ingredients in a small bowl and set aside.

2 Put the rice noodles in a large bowl and pour over enough hot water to cover; leave to stand for 15 minutes until softened. Drain, rinse and drain again.

3 Heat the oil in a heavy-based wok over a high heat until very hot, but not smoking. Add the chicken strips and stir-fry for 1–2 minutes until they just begin to colour. Using a slotted spoon, transfer to a plate. Reduce the heat to medium-high.

4 Stir the shallots, garlic and spring onions into the wok and stir-fry for about 1 minute. Stir in the drained noodles, then the prepared sauce.

5 Return the reserved chicken to the pan with the crabmeat, bean-sprouts and radish; toss well. Cook for about 5 minutes until heated through, tossing frequently. If the noodles begin to stick, add a little water.

6 Turn out on to a serving dish and sprinkle with the chopped roasted peanuts. Garnish with coriander sprigs and serve immediately.

Stir-fried Beef

A quick-and-easy stir-fry for any day of the week, this simple beef recipe is a good one-pan main dish. Serve with a simple green side salad.

NUTRITIONAL INFORMATION

Calories	583	Sugars	........13g
Protein	........40g	Fat	..........22g
Carbohydrate	...59g	Saturates	.......7g

 10 mins   15–20 mins

SERVES 4

I N G R E D I E N T S

1 bunch spring onions

2 tbsp sunflower oil

1 garlic clove, crushed

1 tsp finely fresh ginger root, chopped

500 g/1 lb 2 oz tender beef, cut into
  thin strips

1 large red pepper, deseeded
  and sliced

1 small red chilli, deseeded and chopped

350 g/12 oz/3⅓ cups fresh beansprouts

1 small lemon grass stalk,
  finely chopped

2 tbsp smooth peanut butter

4 tbsp coconut milk

1 tbsp rice vinegar

1 tbsp soy sauce

1 tsp soft light brown sugar

250 g/9 oz medium egg noodles

salt and pepper

1 Trim and thinly slice the spring onions, setting aside some slices to use as a garnish.

2 Heat the oil in a frying pan or wok over a high heat. Add the onions, garlic and ginger and then stir-fry for 2–3 minutes to soften. Add the beef and continue stir-frying for 4–5 minutes until browned evenly.

3 Add the pepper and stir-fry for a further 3–4 minutes. Add the chilli and beansprouts and stir-fry for 2 minutes. Mix together the lemon grass, peanut butter, coconut milk, vinegar, soy sauce and sugar, then stir this mixture into the wok.

4 Meanwhile, cook the egg noodles in boiling, lightly salted water for 4 minutes, or according to the packet directions. Drain and stir into the frying pan or wok, tossing to mix evenly.

5 Adjust seasoning with salt and pepper to taste. Sprinkle the beef and vegetables with the reserved spring onions and serve hot.

Beef Satay

Satay recipes vary throughout the East, but these little beef skewers are a classic version of the traditional dish.

NUTRITIONAL INFORMATION

Calories 489	Sugars 14g
Protein 38g	Fat 31g
Carbohydrate ...17g	Saturates 8g

20 mins, plus marinating time   10–15 mins

SERVES 4

INGREDIENTS

500 g/1 lb 2 oz beef fillet

2 garlic cloves, crushed

2 cm/¾ inch piece fresh ginger root, finely grated

1 tbsp soft light brown sugar

1 tbsp dark soy sauce

1 tbsp lime juice

2 tsp sesame oil

1 tsp ground coriander

1 tsp turmeric

½ tsp chilli powder

chopped cucumber and red pepper, to serve

PEANUT SAUCE

300 ml/10 fl oz coconut milk

8 tbsp crunchy peanut butter

½ small onion, grated

2 tsp soft light brown sugar

½ tsp chilli powder

1 tbsp dark soy sauce

COOK'S TIP

The grill must be very hot to cook the tender beef so quickly it seals in all the juices and flavour.

1 Cut the beef fillets into approximately 1 cm/½ inch cubes and place them in a large bowl.

2 Add the garlic, ginger, sugar, soy sauce, lime juice, sesame oil, ground coriander, turmeric and chilli powder to the bowl. Mix well to coat the pieces of meat evenly. Cover the bowl and leave to marinate in the refrigerator for at least 2 hours, or overnight if possible.

3 To make the peanut sauce, place all the ingredients in a saucepan and stir over a medium heat until boiling. Remove from the heat and keep warm.

4 Thread the beef cubes on to bamboo skewers. Grill the skewers under a preheated grill for 3–5 minutes, turning often, until golden. Alternatively, barbecue over hot coals. Serve with the sauce and cucumber and pepper as garnish.

Beef, Peppers & Lemon Grass

A delicately flavoured stir-fry infused with lemon grass and ginger. Peppers add colour, and it is all cooked within minutes.

NUTRITIONAL INFORMATION

Calories 230	Sugars 4g
Protein 26g	Fat 12g
Carbohydrate 6g	Saturates 3g

 10–15 mins 10 mins

SERVES 4

I N G R E D I E N T S

500 g/1 lb 2 oz lean beef fillet 2 tbsp vegetable oil

1 garlic clove, finely chopped

1 lemon grass stalk, finely shredded

2.5 cm/1 inch piece fresh ginger root, finely chopped

1 red pepper, deseeded and thickly sliced

1 green pepper, deseeded and thickly sliced

1 onion, thickly sliced

2 tbsp lime juice

boiled noodles or rice, to serve

1 Cut the beef into long, thin strips, cutting across the grain.

2 Heat the oil in a large frying pan or wok over a high heat. Add the garlic and stir-fry for 1 minute.

3 Add the beef and stir-fry for a further 2–3 minutes until lightly coloured. Stir in the lemon grass and ginger and remove the wok from the heat.

4 Remove the beef from the fryingpan or wok and keep to one side. Next add the red and green peppers and onion to the pan or wok and stir-fry over a high heat for 2–3 minutes until the onions are just turning golden brown and slightly softened.

5 Return the beef to the pan, stir in the lime juice and season to taste with salt and pepper. Serve with noodles or rice.

COOK'S TIP

When preparing lemon grass, take care to remove the outer layers, which can be tough and fibrous. Use only the centre, tender part, which has the finest flavour.

Hot Beef & Coconut Curry

The heat of the chillies in this red-hot curry is balanced and softened by coconut milk, producing a creamy-textured, rich and lavishly spiced curry.

NUTRITIONAL INFORMATION

Calories 230   Sugars 6g
Protein . . . . .29g   Fat 10g
Carbohydrate . . . .8g   Saturates 3g

 10–15 mins   30–35 mins

SERVES 4

INGREDIENTS

400 ml/14 fl oz coconut milk

2 tbsp Thai red curry paste

2 garlic cloves, crushed

500 g/1lb 2 oz braising steak

2 kaffir lime leaves, shredded

3 tbsp kaffir lime juice

2 tbsp Thai fish sauce

1 large red chilli, deseeded and sliced

½ tsp turmeric

½ tsp salt

2 tbsp fresh basil leaves, chopped

2 tbsp fresh coriander leaves, chopped

shredded coconut, to garnish

boiled rice, to serve

1 Place the coconut milk in a pan and bring to the boil. Lower the heat and simmer for 10 minutes until the milk has thickened. Stir in the curry paste and garlic and simmer for 5 minutes.

2 Cut the beef into 2 cm/³/₄ inch chunks, add to the pan and bring to the boil, stirring. Lower the heat and add lime leaves, and juice, fish sauce, chilli, and turmeric.

3 Cover the pan and continue simmering for 20–25 minutes until the meat is tender, adding a little water if the sauce looks too dry.

4 Stir in the basil and coriander and adjust the seasoning with salt and pepper to taste. Sprinkle with coconut and serve with boiled rice.

COOK'S TIP

Use large, mild red chilli peppers – either fresno or Dutch – because they give more colour to the dish. If you prefer to use small Thai, or bird-eye, chillies, you need only one as they are much hotter.

Roasted Red Pork

This red-glazed, sweet-and-tender pork, of Chinese origin, is a colourful addition to many stir-fries, salads and soups.

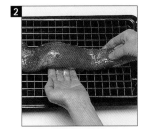

NUTRITIONAL INFORMATION

Calories . . . . . . .276 Sugars 5g
Protein . . . . .34g Fat 13g
Carbohydrate . . . .7g Saturates 4g

10-15 mins, plus marinating

55-60 mins

SERVES 4

INGREDIENTS

600 g/1 lb 5 oz pork fillets

Chinese leaves, shredded to serve

red chilli flower, to garnish

MARINADE

2 garlic cloves, crushed

1 tbsp fresh ginger root, grated

1 tbsp light soy sauce

1 tbsp Thai fish sauce

1 tbsp rice wine

1 tbsp hoi-sin sauce

1 tbsp sesame oil

1 tbsp palm sugar or soft brown sugar

½ tsp five-spice powder

a few drops red food colouring (optional)

1 Mix all the ingredients for the marinade together and spread over the pork, turning to coat evenly. Place in a large dish, cover and leave in the refrigerator to marinate overnight.

2 Place a rack in a roasting tin, then half-fill the tin with boiling water. Lift the pork from the marinade and place on the rack. Reserve the marinade for later use.

3 Roast in a preheated oven at 220°C/ 425°F/Gas Mark 7 for about 20 minutes. Baste with the marinade, then lower the heat to 180°C/350°F/Gas Mark 4 and continue roasting for 35–40 minutes, basting occasionally until the pork is reddish brown and thoroughly cooked.

4 Cut the pork into slices and serve on a bed of shredded Chinese leaves, garnished with a red chilli flower.

COOK'S TIP
The pork may also be grilled. Cut the meat into slices or strips and coat in the marinade, then arrange on a foil-lined grill pan and grill under a high heat, turning occasionally and basting with marinade.

Pork with Sesame Seeds

Thai cooks are fond of adding sweet flavours to meat, as in this unusual pork dish, with soy and garlic to balance the sweetness of the honey.

NUTRITIONAL INFORMATION

Calories 322	Sugars 8g
Protein 35g	Fat 14g
Carbohydrate ...13g	Saturates 4g

15 mins   40–45 mins

SERVES 4

I N G R E D I E N T S

2 pork fillets, about 275 g/9½ oz each

2 tbsp dark soy sauce

2 tbsp clear honey

2 garlic cloves, crushed

1 tbsp sesame seeds

1 onion, thinly sliced in rings

1 tbsp seasoned plain flour

sunflower oil, to fry

crisp salad, to serve

1 Trim the fat off the pork fillets and place them in a wide non-metallic dish.

2 Mix together the soy sauce, clear honey and garlic. Spread this mixture over the pork fillets, turning the meat to coat it evenly.

3 Lift the pork fillets into a roasting tin or shallow ovenproof dish. Sprinkle evenly with sesame seeds.

4 Roast the pork in an oven preheated at 200°C/400°F/Gas Mark 6 for about 20 minutes, spooning over any juices. Cover loosely with foil to prevent over-browning and roast for a further 10–15 minutes until the meat is thoroughly cooked.

5 Meanwhile, dip the onion slices in the flour and shake off the excess. Heat the oil and fry the onion rings until golden and crisp, turning occasionally. Serve the pork in slices with the fried onions on a bed of crisp salad.

COOK'S TIP

This pork is also excellent served cold, and it's a good choice for picnics, especially served with a spicy sambal or chilli relish.

Spicy Fried Minced Pork

A warmly spiced dish, this is ideal for a quick family meal. Just cook fine egg noodles for an accompaniment while the meat sizzles.

NUTRITIONAL INFORMATION

Calories 278   Sugars 4g
Protein ....28g   Fat 16g
Carbohydrate ....7g   Saturates 4g

10 mins   15-20 mins

SERVES 4

I N G R E D I E N T S

2 garlic cloves

3 shallots

2.5 cm/1 inch piece fresh ginger root, finely chopped

2 tbsp sunflower oil

500 g/1 lb 2 oz lean minced pork

2 tbsp Thai fish sauce

1 tbsp dark soy sauce

1 tbsp Thai red curry paste

4 dried kaffir lime leaves, crumbled

4 plum tomatoes, chopped

3 tbsp fresh coriander, chopped

salt and pepper

boiled fine egg noodles, to serve

fresh coriander sprigs, to garnish

1 Peel and finely chop the garlic, shallots and ginger. Heat the oil in a wok over a medium heat. Add the garlic, shallots and ginger and stir-fry for about 2 minutes. Stir in the pork and continue stir-frying until golden brown.

2 Stir in the fish sauce, soy sauce, curry paste and lime leaves, and stir-fry for a further 1–2 minutes over a high heat.

3 Add the tomatoes and cook for a further 5–6 minutes, stirring occasionally.

4 Stir in the chopped coriander and season to taste with salt and pepper. Serve hot, spooned on to boiled fine egg noodles, garnished with coriander sprigs.

COOK'S TIP

Dried kaffir lime leaves can be crumbled easily straight into quick dishes such as this. If you prefer to use fresh kaffir lime leaves, shred them finely and add to the dish.

Red Lamb Curry

This richly spiced curry uses the red-hot chilli flavour of Thai red curry paste, made with dried red chillies, to give it a warm, russet-red colour.

NUTRITIONAL INFORMATION

Calories 363   Sugars 11g
Protein . . . . .29g   Fat 19g
Carbohydrate . . .21g   Saturates 6g

 15-20 mins   30-35 mins

SERVES 4

I N G R E D I E N T S

500 g/1 lb 2 oz boneless lean leg of lamb

2 tbsp vegetable oil

1 large onion, sliced

2 garlic cloves, crushed

2 tbsp Thai red curry paste

150 ml/5 fl oz coconut milk

1 tbsp soft light brown sugar

1 large red pepper, deseeded and thickly sliced

125 ml/4 fl oz lamb or beef stock

1 tbsp Thai fish sauce

2 tbsp lime juice

225 g/8 oz canned water chestnuts, drained

2 tbsp fresh coriander, chopped

2 tbsp fresh basil, chopped

salt and pepper

boiled jasmine rice, to serve

fresh basil leaves, to garnish

COOK'S TIP

This curry can also be made with other lean red meats. Try replacing the lamb with trimmed duck breasts or pieces of lean braising beef.

1 Trim the meat and cut into 3 cm/ 1¼ inch cubes. Heat the oil in a frying pan over a high heat and fry the onion and garlic for 2–3 minutes to soften. Add the meat and fry until lightly browned.

2 Stir in the curry paste and cook for a few seconds, then add the coconut milk and sugar and bring to the boil. Reduce the heat and simmer for 15 minutes, stirring occasionally.

3 Stir in the red pepper, stock, fish sauce and lime juice, cover and continue simmering for a further 15 minutes, or until the meat is tender.

4 Add the water chestnuts, coriander and basil, adjust the seasoning to taste. Serve with jasmine rice garnished with fresh basil leaves.

Chicken & Mango Stir-Fry

A colourful, exotic mix of flavours that works surprisingly well, this dish is easy and quick to cook – ideal for a mid-week family meal.

NUTRITIONAL INFORMATION

Calories 200   Sugars 5g
Protein ....23g   Fat 6g
Carbohydrate ....7g   Saturates 1g

 15 mins   10–15 mins

SERVES 4

I N G R E D I E N T S

6 boneless, skinless chicken thighs

2.5 cm/1 inch piece fresh ginger
  root, grated

1 garlic clove, crushed

1 small red chilli, deseeded

1 large red pepper

4 spring onions

200 g/7 oz mangetout

100 g/3½ oz baby sweetcorn cobs

1 large, firm, ripe mango

2 tbsp sunflower oil

1 tbsp light soy sauce

3 tbsp rice wine or sherry

1 tsp sesame oil

salt and pepper

sliced chives, to garnish

1 Cut the chicken into long, thin strips and place them in a bowl. Mix together the ginger, garlic and chilli, then add the mixture to the chicken strips stirring to coat them evenly.

2 Slice the red pepper thinly, cutting diagonally. Trim and diagonally slice the spring onions. Cut the mangetout and sweetcorn cobs in half diagonally. Peel the mango, remove the stone and slice thinly.

3 Heat the sunfloweroil in a large frying pan or wok over a high heat. Add the chicken slices and stir-fry for 4–5 minutes until just turning golden brown. Add the sliced red peppers and stir-fry over a medium heat for about 4–5 minutes to soften them.

4 Add the sliced spring onions, mangetout and sweetcorn cobs and stir-fry for a further minute.

5 Mix together the soy sauce, rice wine or sherry and sesame oil and stir it into the wok. Add the mango and stir gently for 1 minute to heat thoroughly.

6 Adjust the seasoning with salt and pepper to taste and serve immediately. Garnish with chives.

Thai Coriander Chicken

These simple marinated chicken breasts are packed with powerful, zesty flavours, and are best accompanied by a simple dish of plain boiled rice.

NUTRITIONAL INFORMATION

Calories 171   Sugars 8g
Protein . . . . .31g   Fat 2g
Carbohydrate . . . .9g   Saturates 0.5g

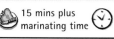

15 mins plus marinating time   15–20 mins

SERVES 4

INGREDIENTS

4 boneless chicken breasts, without skin

2 garlic cloves, peeled

1 fresh green chilli, deseeded

2 cm/¾ inch piece fresh ginger root, peeled

4 tbsp fresh coriander, chopped

rind of 1 lime, finely grated

3 tbsp lime juice

2 tbsp light soy sauce

1 tbsp caster sugar

175 ml/6 fl oz coconut milk

plain boiled rice, to serve

cucumber and radish slices, to garnish

1 Using a sharp knife, cut 3 deep slashes into the skinned side of each chicken breast. Place the breasts in a single layer in a wide, non-metallic dish.

2 Put the garlic, chilli, ginger, coriander, lime rind and juice, soy sauce, caster sugar and coconut milk in a food processor and process until a smooth purée forms.

3 Spread the purée over both sides of the chicken breasts, coating them evenly. Cover the dish and leave the mixture to marinate in the refrigerator for about 1 hour.

4 Lift the chicken from the marinade, drain off the excess and place in a grill pan. Grill under a preheated grill for 12–15 minutes until thoroughly and evenly cooked.

5 Meanwhile, place the remaining marinade in a saucepan and bring to the boil. Lower the heat and simmer for several minutes to heat thoroughly. Serve with the chicken breasts, accompanied with rice and garnished with cucumber and radish slices.

Green Chicken Curry

Thai curries are traditionally very hot, and designed to make a little go a long way – the thin, highly spiced juices are eaten with lots of rice.

NUTRITIONAL INFORMATION

Calories 193	Sugars 9g	
Protein 22g	Fat 8g	
Carbohydrate 9g	Saturates 1g	

 10 mins   45–50 mins

SERVES 4

INGREDIENTS

6 boneless, skinless chicken thighs

400 ml/14 fl oz coconut milk

2 garlic cloves, crushed

2 tbsp Thai fish sauce

2 tbsp Thai green curry paste

12 baby aubergines, also called Thai pea aubergines

3 green chillies, finely chopped

3 kaffir lime leaves, shredded

4 tbsp fresh coriander, chopped

boiled rice, to serve

1 Cut the chicken into bite-sized pieces. Pour the coconut milk into a large fryingpan or wok over a high heat and bring to the boil.

2 Add the chicken pieces, garlic and fish sauce to the frying pan and bring back to the boil. Lower the heat and simmer gently for about 30 minutes, or until the chicken is just tender.

3 Remove the chicken from the mixture with a perforated spoon. Set aside and keep warm.

4 Stir the green curry paste into the pan, add the aubergines, chillies and lime leaves and simmer for 5 minutes.

5 Return the chicken to the frying pan and bring to the boil. Adjust the seasoning to taste with salt and pepper, then stir in the coriander. Serve the curry with boiled rice.

COOK'S TIP

Baby or 'pea aubergines' as the Thais call them, are traditionally used in this curry. If you cannot find them in an oriental food shop, use chopped ordinary aubergine or substitute a few green peas.

Glazed Duck Breasts

Duck is excellent cooked with strong flavours, and when it is marinated and coated in this rich, dark, sticky oriental glaze, it is irresistible.

NUTRITIONAL INFORMATION

Calories 264   Sugars 1g
Protein ....30g   Fat 11g
Carbohydrate ...13g   Saturates 3g

20 mins, plus marinating time   10–15 mins

SERVES 4

INGREDIENTS

4 boneless duck breasts

2 garlic cloves, crushed

4 tsp light soft brown sugar

3 tbsp lime juice

1 tbsp soy sauce

1 tsp chilli sauce

1 tsp vegetable oil

2 tbsp plum jam

125 ml/4 fl oz chicken stock

salt and pepper

1 Using a small, sharp knife, cut deep slashes in the skin of the duck to make a diamond pattern. Place the duck breasts in a wide, non-metallic dish.

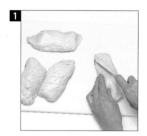

2 Mix together the garlic, sugar, lime juice, soy and chilli sauces, then spoon over the duck breasts, turning well to coat them evenly. Cover the dish with plastic wrap and leave to marinate in the refrigerator for at least 3 hours, or overnight.

3 Drain the duck, reserving the marinade. Heat a large, heavy-based pan until very hot and brush with the oil. Add the duck breasts, skin side down, and cook for about 5 minutes or until the skin is browned and crisp. Tip away the excess fat. Turn the duck breasts over.

4 Continue cooking on the other side for 2–3 minutes to brown. Add the reserved marinade, plum jam and stock and simmer for 2 minutes. Adjust the seasoning to taste and serve hot, with the juices spooned over.

COOK'S TIP

If you prefer to reduce the overall fat content of this dish, remove the skin from the duck breasts before cooking and reduce the cooking time slightly.

Crispy Duck with Noodles

A robustly flavoured dish that makes a substantial main course. Serve it with a refreshing cucumber salad or a light vegetable stir-fry.

NUTRITIONAL INFORMATION

Calories ....433 Sugars 7g
Protein ....25g Fat 10g
Carbohydrate ...59g Saturates 2g

15 mins, plus marinating time   20–25 mins

SERVES 4

INGREDIENTS

3 duck breasts, total weight about 400 g/14 oz

2 garlic cloves, crushed

1½ tsp chilli paste

1 tbsp honey

3 tbsp dark soy sauce

½ tsp five-spice powder

250 g/9 oz rice stick noodles

1 tsp vegetable oil

1 tsp sesame oil

2 spring onion, sliced

100 g/3½ oz mangetout

2 tbsp tamarind juice

sesame seeds, to garnish

1 Prick the duck breast skin all over with a fork and place in a deep dish.

2 Mix together the garlic, chilli, honey, soy sauce and five-spice powder, then pour over the duck. Turn the breasts over to coat them evenly, then cover and leave to marinate in the refrigerator for at least 1 hour.

3 Meanwhile, soak the rice noodles in hot water for 15 minutes. Drain well.

4 Drain the duck breasts from the marinade and grill on a rack under high heat for about 10 minutes, turning them over occasionally, until they become a rich golden brown. Remove and slice the duck breasts thinly.

5 Heat the vegetable and sesame oils in a frying pan and toss the spring onions and mangetout for 2 minutes. Stir in the reserved marinade and tamarind juice and bring to the boil.

6 Add the sliced duck and noodles to the frying pan and toss to heat thoroughly. Serve immediately, sprinkled with sesame seeds.

Thai Green Fish Curry

This pale green curry paste can be used as the basis for a range of Thai dishes. It is also delicious with chicken and beef.

NUTRITIONAL INFORMATION

Calories	217	Sugars	.........3g
Protein	........12g	Fat	..........17g
Carbohydrate	....5g	Saturates	......10g

20 mins   15 mins

SERVES 4

INGREDIENTS

2 tbsp vegetable oil

1 garlic clove, chopped

1 small aubergine, diced

125 ml/4 fl oz coconut cream

2 tbsp Thai fish sauce

1 tsp sugar

225 g/8 oz firm white fish, cut into pieces, such as cod, haddock, halibut

125 ml/4 fl oz fish stock

2 lime leaves, finely shredded

about 15 leaves Thai basil, if available, or ordinary basil

plain boiled rice or noodles, to serve

GREEN CURRY PASTE

5 green chillies, deseeded and chopped

2 tsp chopped lemon grass

1 large shallot, chopped

2 garlic cloves, chopped

1 tsp freshly grated ginger or galangal, if available

2 coriander roots, chopped

½ tsp ground coriander

¼ tsp ground cumin

1 kaffir lime leaf, finely chopped

1 tsp shrimp paste (optional)

½ tsp salt

1 Make the curry paste. Put all the ingredients into a blender and blend to a paste, add a little water if necessary. Alternatively, pound the ingredients in a mortar and pestle. Set aside.

2 In a frying pan, heat the oil until almost smoking and add the garlic. Fry until golden. Add the curry paste and stir-fry a few seconds. Add the aubergine. Stir-fry for 4–5 minutes until soft.

3 Add the coconut cream. Bring to the boil and stir until the cream thickens and curdles slightly. Add the fish sauce and sugar to the frying pan and stir well.

4 Add the fish pieces and stock. Simmer for 3–4 minutes, stirring occasionally, until the fish is just tender. Add the lime leaves and basil, and then cook for a further minute. Serve with plain boiled rice or noodles.

Red Prawn Curry

Like all Thai curries, this one has as its base a paste of chillies and spices and a sauce of coconut milk.

NUTRITIONAL INFORMATION

Calories	149	Sugars	.........4g
Protein	........15g	Fat	...........7g
Carbohydrate	....6g	Saturates	.......1g

 15–20 mins   15–20 mins

SERVES 4

INGREDIENTS

2 tbsp vegetable oil

1 garlic clove, finely chopped

1 tbsp red curry paste

200 ml/7 fl oz coconut milk

2 tbsp Thai fish sauce

1 tsp sugar

12 large raw prawns, de-veined

2 lime leaves, finely shredded

1 small red chilli, deseeded and finely sliced

10 leaves Thai basil, if available, or ordinary basil

RED CURRY PASTE

3 dried long red chillies

½ tsp ground coriander

¼ tsp ground cumin

½ tsp ground black pepper

2 garlic cloves, chopped

2 lemon grass stalks, chopped

1 kaffir lime leaf, finely chopped

1 tsp freshly grated ginger root or galangal, if available

1 tsp shrimp paste (optional)

½ tsp salt

1 Make the red curry paste. Put all the ingredients in a blender and blend to a paste, add a little water if necessary. Alternatively, pound the ingredients in a mortar and pestle. Set aside.

2 Heat the oil in a wok or frying pan until almost smoking. Add the garlic and fry until golden. Add 1 tablespoon of the curry paste and cook for a further minute. Add half the coconut milk, fish sauce and sugar. Stir well. The mixture should thicken slightly.

3 Add the prawns and simmer for 3–4 minutes until they turn colour. Add the remaining coconut milk, the lime leaves and chilli. Cook a further 2–3 minutes until the prawns are just tender.

4 Add the basil leaves, stir until wilted and serve immediately.

Coconut Rice & Monkfish

This is a delicious Thai-influenced recipe of rice, cooked in coconut milk, with spicy grilled monkfish and fresh peas.

NUTRITIONAL INFORMATION

Calories 440   Sugars 8g
Protein ....22g   Fat 14g
Carbohydrate ...60g   Saturates 2g

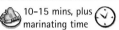

10–15 mins, plus marinating time   35 mins

SERVES 4

I N G R E D I E N T S

1 hot red chilli, deseeded and chopped

1 tsp crushed chilli flakes

2 garlic cloves, chopped

2 pinches saffron

3 tbsp roughly chopped mint leaves

4 tbsp olive oil

2 tbsp lemon juice

375 g/12 oz monkfish fillet, cut into
   bite-sized pieces

1 onion, finely chopped

225 g/8 oz long grain rice

400 g/14 oz canned chopped tomatoes

200 ml/7 fl oz coconut milk

115 g/4 oz peas

salt and pepper

2 tbsp chopped fresh coriander, to garnish

1   In a food processor or blender, blend together the fresh and dried chilli, garlic, saffron, mint, olive oil and lemon juice until finely chopped but not smooth.

2   Put the monkfish into a non-metallic dish and pour over the spice paste, mixing together well. Set aside for 20 minutes to marinate.

3   Heat a large saucepan until very hot. Using a slotted spoon, lift the monkfish from the marinade and add in batches to the hot pan. Cook for 3–4 minutes until browned and firm. Remove with a slotted spoon and set aside.

4   Add the onion and remaining marinade to the same pan and cook for 5 minutes until softened and lightly browned. Add the rice and stir until well coated. Add the tomatoes and coconut milk. Bring to the boil, cover and simmer very gently for 15 minutes. Stir in the peas, season and arrange the fish over the top. Cover and continue to cook over a very low heat for 5 minutes. Serve garnished with the chopped coriander.

Steamed Yellow Fish Fillets

Thailand has an abundance of fresh fish, which is an important part of the local diet. Dishes such as these steamed fillets are very popular.

NUTRITIONAL INFORMATION

Calories	165	Sugars	.........1g
Protein	........23g	Fat	...........2g
Carbohydrate	...13g	Saturates	.......1g

15-20 mins   12-15 mins

SERVES 4

INGREDIENTS

500 g/1 lb 2 oz firm fish fillets, such as red snapper, sole or monkfish

1 dried red bird-eye chilli

1 small onion, chopped

3 garlic cloves, chopped

2 sprigs fresh coriander

1 tsp coriander seeds

½ tsp turmeric

½ tsp ground black pepper

1 tbsp Thai fish sauce

2 tbsp coconut milk

1 small egg, beaten

2 tbsp rice flour

red and green chilli strips, to garnish

soy sauce, to serve

1 Remove any skin from the fish and cut the fillets diagonally into long 2 cm/¾ inch wide strips.

2 Place the dried chilli, onion, garlic, fresh coriander and coriander seeds in a pestle and mortar and grind until it is a smooth paste.

3 Add the turmeric, pepper, fish sauce, coconut milk and beaten egg, stirring well to mix evenly.

4 Dip the fish strips into the paste mixture, then into the rice flour to coat lightly.

5 Bring the water in the bottom of a steamer to the boil, then arrange the fish strips in the top of the steamer. Cover and steam for about 12–15 minutes until the fish is just firm.

6 Garnish the fish with chilli strips and serve with soy sauce and an accompaniment of stir-fried vegetables or salad.

COOK'S TIP

If you don't have a steamer, improvise by placing a large metal colander over a large pan of boiling water and cover with an upturned plate to enclose the fish as it steams.

Baked Fish with Chilli Sauce

Almost any whole fish can be cooked by this method, but snapper, sea bass or John Dory are particularly good with the Thai flavours.

NUTRITIONAL INFORMATION

Calories 267	Sugars 9g	
Protein 38g	Fat 8g	
Carbohydrate 11g	Saturates 2g	

10-15 mins   40-45 mins

SERVES 4

INGREDIENTS

handful of fresh sweet basil leaves

750 g/1 lb 10 oz whole red snapper, sea bass or John Dory, cleaned

2 tbsp groundnut oil

2 tbsp Thai fish sauce

2 garlic cloves, crushed

1 tsp galangal or ginger root, finely grated

2 large fresh red chillies, sliced diagonally

1 yellow pepper, deseeded and diced

1 tbsp palm sugar

1 tbsp rice vinegar

2 tbsp water or fish stock

2 tomatoes, deseeded and sliced into thin wedges

1 Reserve a few fresh basil leaves for garnish and tuck the rest inside the body cavity of the fish.

COOK'S TIP

Large red chillies are less hot than the tiny red bird-eye chillies, so you can use them more freely in cooked dishes such as this for a mild heat. Remove the seeds if you prefer.

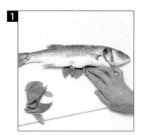

2 Heat 1 tablespoon oil in a frying pan and fry the fish quickly to brown, turning once. Place the fish on a piece of foil in a roasting tin and spoon over the fish sauce. Wrap the foil over the fish loosely. Bake at 190°C/375°F/Gas Mark 5 for 25–30 minutes until just cooked.

3 Meanwhile, heat the remaining oil and fry the garlic, galangal and chillies for 30 seconds. Add the pepper and stir-fry for a further 2–3 minutes to soften.

4 Stir in the sugar, vinegar and water, then add the tomatoes and bring to the boil. Remove the pan from the heat.

5 Transfer the fish to a warmed serving plate. Add the fish juices to the pan, then spoon the sauce over the fish and scatter with the reserved basil leaves.

Curry-coated Baked Cod

An easy, economical main dish which can transform any white fish into an exotic meal.

NUTRITIONAL INFORMATION

Calories	223	Sugars	.........1g
Protein	........31g	Fat	...........4g
Carbohydrate	...16g	Saturates	.....0.1g

10-15 mins   35-40 mins

SERVES 4

I N G R E D I E N T S

½ tsp sesame oil

4 pieces cod fillet, about 150 g/5½ oz each

80 g/3 oz fresh white breadcrumbs

2 tbsp blanched almonds, chopped

2 tsp Thai green curry paste

rind of ½ lime, finely grated

salt and pepper

boiled new potatoes, to serve

lime slices and rind and mixed
    green leaves, to garnish

1 Brush the sesame oil over the base of a wide, shallow ovenproof dish or baking tin, then place the pieces of cod in a single layer.

2 Mix the fresh breadcrumbs, almonds, curry paste and lime rind together, stirring well to blend thoroughly and evenly. Season to taste with salt and pepper.

3 Carefully spoon the crumb mixture over the fish pieces, pressing lightly to hold it in place.

4 Place the dish, uncovered, in a preheated oven at 200°C/400°F/Gas Mark 6 and bake for 35–40 minutes until the fish is cooked through and the crumb topping is golden brown.

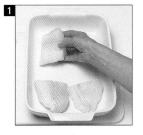

5 Serve the dish hot, garnished with lime slices and lime rind and mixed green leaves and accompanied with boiled new potatoes.

COOK'S TIP

To test whether the fish is cooked through, use a fork to pierce it in the thickest part – if the flesh is white all the way through and flakes apart easily, the fish is cooked sufficiently.

Sweet & Sour Tuna

Tuna is a firm, meaty-textured fish which is abundant in the seas around Thailand. You can also use shark or mackerel in this dish.

NUTRITIONAL INFORMATION

Calories 303	Sugars 12g	
Protein 31g	Fat 12g	
Carbohydrate ...20g	Saturates 3g	

 10 mins   15–20 mins

SERVES 4

INGREDIENTS

4 fresh tuna steaks, about 500 g/ 1 lb 2 oz total weight

¼ tsp ground black pepper

2 tbsp groundnut oil

1 onion, diced

1 small red pepper, deseeded and cut into matchsticks

1 garlic clove, crushed

½ cucumber, deseeded and cut into matchsticks

2 pineapple slices, diced

1 tsp fresh ginger root, finely chopped

1 tbsp soft light brown sugar

1 tbsp cornflour

1½ tbsp lime juice

1 tbsp Thai fish sauce

250 ml/9 fl oz fish stock

lime and cucumber slices, to garnish

1 Sprinkle the tuna steaks with pepper on both sides. Heat a heavy frying pan or griddle and brush with a little of the oil. Arrange the tuna on the griddle and cook for about 8 minutes, turning them over once.

2 Heat the remaining oil in another frying pan and fry the onion, pepper and garlic gently for 3–4 minutes to soften.

3 Remove from the heat and stir in the cucumber, pineapple, ginger and sugar.

4 Blend the cornflour with the lime juice and fish sauce, then stir into the stock and add to the pan. Stir over a medium heat until boiling, then cook for 1–2 minutes until thickened and clear.

5 Spoon the sauce over the tuna and serve garnished with lime slices and cucumber.

COOK'S TIP

Tuna can be served quite lightly cooked; it can become too dry if it is overcooked.

Thai-spiced Salmon

Marinated in delicate Thai spices and quickly pan-fried to perfection, these salmon fillets are ideal for a special dinner.

NUTRITIONAL INFORMATION

Calories	329	Sugars	.......0.1g
Protein	........30g	Fat	..........23g
Carbohydrate	...0.1g	Saturates	.......4g

 10 mins, plus marinating time   4–5 mins

SERVES 4

I N G R E D I E N T S

2.5 cm/1 in piece fresh ginger root, grated

1 tsp coriander seeds, crushed

¼ tsp chilli powder

1 tbsp lime juice

1 tsp sesame oil

4 pieces salmon fillet with skin, about 150 g/5½ oz each

2 tbsp vegetable oil

boiled rice and stir-fried vegetables, to serve

1 Mix together the grated ginger, crushed coriander, chilli powder, lime juice and sesame oil.

2 Place the salmon on a wide, non-metallic plate or dish and spoon the mixture over the flesh side of the fillets, spreading it to coat each piece of salmon evenly.

3 Cover the dish with cling film and chill the salmon in the refrigerator for 30 minutes.

4 Heat a wide, heavy-based frying pan or griddle pan with the oil over a high heat. Place the salmon on the hot pan or griddle, skin side down.

5 Cook the salmon for 4–5 minutes, without turning, until the salmon is crusty underneath and the flesh flakes easily. Serve at once with the boiled rice and stir-fried vegetables.

COOK'S TIP

Use a heavy-based pan or solid griddle for this recipe, so the fish cooks evenly throughout without sticking. If it is very thick, turn it over carefully to cook on the other side for 2–3 minutes.

Salmon with Red Curry

Banana leaves are widely used in Thai cooking to wrap raw ingredients such as fish before baking or steaming.

NUTRITIONAL INFORMATION

Calories 351	Sugars 6g	
Protein 36g	Fat 20g	
Carbohydrate 6g	Saturates 3g	

15 mins   15–20 mins

SERVES 4

INGREDIENTS

4 salmon steaks, about 175 g/6 oz each

2 banana leaves, halved

1 garlic clove, crushed

1 tsp fresh ginger root, grated

1 tbsp Thai red curry paste

1 tsp soft light brown sugar

1 tbsp Thai fish sauce

2 tbsp lime juice

TO GARNISH

lime wedges

finely chopped red chilli

1 Place a salmon steak on the centre of each half banana leaf.

2 Mix the garlic, ginger, curry paste, sugar and fish sauce. Spread over the fish and sprinkle with lime juice.

3 Wrap the banana leaves around the fish, tucking in the sides as you go to make a neat, compact bundle.

4 Place the parcels seam side down on a baking sheet and bake in a preheated oven at 220°C/425°F/Gas Mark 7 for 15–20 minutes until the fish is cooked and the banana leaves are beginning to brown. Serve garnished with lime wedges and chilli.

COOK'S TIP

Fresh banana leaves are often sold in packs containing several leaves, but if you buy more than you need, they will store in the refrigerator for about a week.

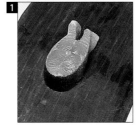

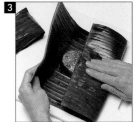

Squid with Hot Sauce

Quick stir-frying is ideal for squid, because if overcooked it can be tough. The technique also seals in the natural colours and flavours.

NUTRITIONAL INFORMATION

Calories 245	Sugars 7g
Protein 32g	Fat 7g
Carbohydrate . . .13g	Saturates 1g

 15 mins 5-10 mins

SERVES 4

INGREDIENTS

750 g/1 lb 10 oz squid, cleaned

1 large red pepper, deseeded

85 g/3 oz mangetout, trimmed

1 head pak choi

3 tbsp black bean sauce

1 tbsp Thai fish sauce

1 tbsp rice wine

1 tbsp dark soy sauce

1 tsp soft light brown sugar

1 tsp cornflour

1 tbsp water

1 tbsp sunflower oil

1 tsp sesame oil

1 small red bird-eye chilli, chopped

1 garlic clove, finely chopped

1 tsp fresh ginger root, grated

2 spring onions, chopped

1 Cut the tentacles from the squid and discard. Cut the body cavities into quarters lengthways. Use the tip of a small sharp knife to score a diamond pattern into the flesh, without cutting all the way through. Pat dry with kitchen paper.

2 Cut the pepper into long, thin slices. Cut the mangetout in half diagonally. Coarsely shred the pak choi.

3 Mix together the black bean sauce, fish sauce, rice wine, soy sauce and sugar. Blend the cornflour with the water and stir into the other sauce ingredients. Keep to one side.

4 Heat the sunflower oil and sesame oil in a wok. Add the chilli, garlic, ginger and spring onions and stir-fry for about 1 minute. Add the pepper and stir-fry for about 2 minutes.

5 Add the squid and stir-fry over a high heat for a further minute. Stir in the mangetout and pak choi, and stir fry for a further minute until wilted.

6 Stir in the sauce ingredients and cook, stirring constantly, for about 2 minutes, until the sauce clears and thickens. Serve immediately.

Scallops with Lime & Chilli

Really fresh scallops have a delicate flavour and texture, needing only minimal cooking, as in this simple stir-fry.

NUTRITIONAL INFORMATION

Calories ....145 Sugars 1g
Protein ....17g Fat 7g
Carbohydrate ....4g Saturates 3g

15 mins   7–8 mins

SERVES 4

I N G R E D I E N T S

16 large scallops

1 tbsp butter

1 tbsp vegetable oil

1 tsp garlic, crushed

1 tsp fresh ginger root, grated

1 bunch spring onions,
   finely sliced

rind of 1 kaffir lime, finely grated

1 small red chilli, deseeded and very
   finely chopped

3 tbsp kaffir lime juice

salt and pepper

lime wedges and boiled rice, to serve

1 Trim the scallops to remove any black intestine. Wash and pat dry. Separate the corals from the white parts. Slice each white part in half, making 2 rounds.

2 Heat the butter and oil in a frying pan or wok. Add the garlic and ginger and stir-fry for 1 minute without browning. Add the spring onions and stir-fry for a further minute.

3 Add the scallops to the frying pan or wok and continue stir-frying over a high heat for 4–5 minutes. Stir in the lime rind, chilli and lime juice and cook for a further minute.

4 Serve the scallops hot, with the juices spooned over them, accompanied by lime wedges and boiled rice.

COOK'S TIP

If fresh scallops are not available, frozen ones can be used, but make sure they are thoroughly defrosted before you cook them. Drain off all excess moisture and pat the scallops dry with kitchen paper.

Spicy Prawn Skewers

Whole tiger prawns cook very quickly on a barbecue or under a grill, so they are ideal for summertime cooking, indoors or outside.

NUTRITIONAL INFORMATION

Calories	106	Sugars	8g
Protein	11g	Fat	3g
Carbohydrate	8g	Saturates	1g

15-20 mins, plus marinating time   5-6 mins

SERVES 4

INGREDIENTS

1 garlic clove, chopped

1 red bird-eye chilli, deseeded and chopped

1 tbsp tamarind paste

1 tbsp sesame oil

1 tbsp dark soy sauce

2 tbsp lime juice

1 tbsp soft light brown sugar

16 large whole raw tiger prawns

crusty bread, lime wedges and salad leaves, to serve

1 Put the garlic, chilli, tamarind paste, sesame oil, soy sauce, lime juice and sugar in a small pan. Stir over a low heat until the sugar is dissolved, then remove from the heat and allow to cool completely.

2 Wash and dry the prawns and place in a single layer in a wide, non-metallic dish. Spoon the marinade over the prawns and turn them over to coat evenly. Cover the dish and leave in the refrigerator to marinate for at least 2 hours, or preferably overnight.

3 Meanwhile, soak 4 bamboo or wooden skewers in water for about 20 minutes. Drain and thread 4 prawns on to each skewer.

4 Grill the skewers under a preheated hot grill for 5–6 minutes, turning them over once, until they turn pink and begin to brown. Alternatively, you can barbecue the prawn skewers over hot coals.

5 Thread a wedge of lime on to the end of each skewer and serve with crusty bread and green salad leaves.

Thai Potato Stir-Fry

This vegetable dish has a traditional sweet and sour Thai flavouring. Tender vegetables are stir-fried with spices and coconut milk.

NUTRITIONAL INFORMATION

Calories 138	Sugars 5g
Protein 2g	Fat 6g
Carbohydrate 1g	Saturates 1g

    15-20 mins   15 mins

SERVES 4

INGREDIENTS

4 waxy potatoes, diced

2 tbsp vegetable oil

1 yellow pepper, diced

1 red pepper, diced

1 carrot, cut into matchstick strips

1 courgette, cut into matchstick strips

2 garlic cloves, crushed

1 red chilli, sliced

1 bunch spring onions,
   halved lengthways

8 tbsp coconut milk

1 tsp chopped lemon grass

2 tsp lime juice

finely grated rind of 1 lime

1 tbsp chopped fresh coriander

 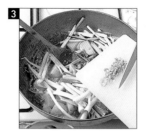 

1 Cook the diced potatoes in a saucepan of boiling water for 5 minutes. Drain thoroughly.

2 Heat the oil in a wok or large frying pan and add the potatoes, diced peppers, carrot, courgette, garlic and chilli. Stir-fry the vegetables for 2-3 minutes.

3 Stir in the spring onions, coconut milk, chopped lemon grass and lime juice and stir-fry the mixture for a further 5 minutes.

4 Add the lime rind and coriander and stir-fry for 1 minute. Serve hot.

COOK'S TIP

Check that the potatoes are not overcooked in step 1, otherwise the potato pieces will disintegrate when they are stir-fried in the wok.

Thai-style Caesar Salad

This simple salad uses fried rice paper wrappers as crispy croûtons. The Thai fish sauce gives the dressing an unusual flavour.

NUTRITIONAL INFORMATION

Calories . . . . . . .533 Sugars 7g
Protein . . . . .4g Fat 43g
Carbohydrate . . .35g Saturates 5g

 10–15 mins   2–5 mins

SERVES 4

INGREDIENTS

1 large head cos lettuce, with outer leaves removed, or 2 hearts

vegetable oil, for deep frying

4–6 large rice paper wrappers or 120 g/4 oz rice paper flakes

small bunch of coriander, leaves stripped from stems

DRESSING

80 ml/3 fl oz rice vinegar

2–3 tbsp Thai fish sauce

2 garlic cloves, coarsely chopped

1 tbsp sugar

2.5 cm/1 inch piece fresh ginger root, peeled and coarsely chopped

125 ml/4 fl oz sunflower oil

salt and pepper

1 Tear the lettuce leaves into bite-sized pieces and put in a large salad bowl.

2 To make the salad dressing, put the rice vinegar, fish sauce, garlic, sugar and ginger in a food processor and process for 15–30 seconds.

3 With the machine running, pour in the sunflower oil slowly until a creamy liquid forms. Season to taste and pour the dressing into a jug; set aside.

4 Heat about 7.5 cm/3 inches of vegetable oil in a deep-fat fryer to 190°C/375°F.

5 Meanwhile, break the rice wrappers into bite-sized pieces and dip each into a bowl of water to soften. Lay on a clean tea towel and pat completely dry.

6 Working in batches, add the rice paper pieces to the hot oil and fry for about 15 seconds until crisp and golden. Using a slotted spoon, transfer to kitchen paper to drain.

7 Add the coriander leaves to the lettuce and toss to mix. Add the fried rice paper 'crisps' and drizzle over the dressing. Toss to coat the salad leaves and serve immediately.

Thai Noodle & Prawn Salad

This delicious combination of rice noodles and prawns, lightly dressed with Thai flavours, makes an impressive first course or a light lunch.

NUTRITIONAL INFORMATION

Calories	204	Sugars	.........8g
Protein	........15g	Fat	..........3g
Carbohydrate	...29g	Saturates	.......1g

 10–15 mins   5 mins

SERVES 4

INGREDIENTS

80 g/3 oz rice vermicelli or rice sticks

175 g/6 oz mangetout, cut crossways in half, if large

5 tbsp lime juice

4 tbsp Thai fish sauce

1 tbsp sugar, or to taste

2.5 cm/1 inch piece fresh ginger root, peeled and finely chopped

1 fresh red chilli, deseeded and thinly sliced on the diagonal

4 tbsp chopped fresh coriander or mint, plus extra for garnishing

10 cm/4 inch piece of cucumber, peeled, deseeded and diced

2 spring onions, thinly sliced on the diagonal

16–20 large cooked, peeled prawns

2 tbsp chopped unsalted peanuts or cashews (optional)

4 whole cooked prawns and lemon slices, to garnish

COOK'S TIP

There are many sizes of rice noodle available – make sure you use the very thin rice noodles, called rice vermicelli or rice sticks or sen mee, otherwise the salad will be too heavy.

1 Put the rice noodles in a large bowl and pour over enough hot water to cover. Stand for about 4 minutes until soft. Drain and rinse under cold running water; drain and set aside.

2 Bring a saucepan of water to the boil. Add the mangetout and return to the boil. Simmer for 1 minute. Drain, rinse under cold running water until cold, then drain and set aside.

3 In a large bowl, whisk together the lime juice, fish sauce, sugar, ginger, chilli and coriander. Stir in the cucumber and spring onions. Add the drained noodles, mangetout and prawns. Toss the salad gently together.

4 Divide the noodle salad among 4 large plates. Sprinkle with chopped coriander and the peanuts (if using), then garnish each plate with a whole prawn and a lemon slice. Serve immediately.

Thai Seafood Salad

This delicious sea food salad, which includes mussels, prawns and squid, is best served chilled.

NUTRITIONAL INFORMATION

Calories	310	Sugars	.........4g
Protein	........30g	Fat	..........18g
Carbohydrate	....7g	Saturates	.......3g

 20 mins, plus chilling time   10–15 mins

SERVES 4

INGREDIENTS

450 g/1 lb live mussels

8 raw tiger prawns

350 g/12 oz squid, cleaned and sliced widthways into rings

115 g/4 oz cooked peeled prawns

½ red onion, finely sliced

½ red (bell) pepper, deseeded and finely sliced

115 g/4 oz/1 cup beansprouts

115 g/4 oz shredded pak choy (Chinese cabbage)

DRESSING

1 garlic clove, crushed

1 tsp grated fresh ginger root

1 red chilli, deseeded and finely chopped

2 tbsp chopped fresh coriander

1 tbsp lime juice

1 tsp finely grated lime rind

1 tbsp light soy sauce

5 tbsp sunflower or groundnut oil

2 tsp sesame oil

salt and pepper

1 Scrub the mussel shells and remove any beards. Place in a saucepan water clinging to the shells. Cook over a high heat for 3–4 minutes, shaking, until all mussels are open. Discard any that remain closed. Strain, reserving the liquid, and refresh under cold water. Drain and set aside.

2 Bring the reserved poaching liquid to the boil and add the prawns. Simmer for 5 minutes. Add the squid and cook for 2 minutes until the shellfish are cooked through. Remove with a slotted spoon and plunge into cold water. Reserve the poaching liquid. Drain the prawns and squid.

3 Remove the mussels from their shells and put into a bowl with the tiger prawns, squid and cooked peeled prawns. Refrigerate for 1 hour.

4 For the dressing, put all the ingredients, except the oils, into a blender and blend to a smooth paste. Add the oils, reserved poaching liquid, seasoning and 4 tbsp cold water. Blend again to combine.

5 Combine the onion, red pepper, beansprouts and pak choy in a bowl and toss with 2–3 tbsp of dressing. Arrange the vegetables on a serving plate. Toss the seafood in the remaining dressing to coat and add to the vegetables. Serve at once.

Warm Tuna Salad

A colourful, refreshing first course that is perfect to make for a special summer lunch or dinner. The dressing can be made in advance.

NUTRITIONAL INFORMATION

Calories	127	Sugars	.........4g
Protein	........13g	Fat	...........5g
Carbohydrate	....6g	Saturates	.......1g

 20 mins   10–15 mins

SERVES 4

INGREDIENTS

50 g/1¾ oz Chinese leaves, shredded

3 tbsp rice wine

2 tbsp Thai fish sauce

1 tbsp fresh ginger root, finely shredded

1 garlic clove, finely chopped

½ small red bird-eye chilli, finely chopped

2 tsp soft light brown sugar

2 tbsp lime juice

400 g/14 oz fresh tuna steak

sunflower oil for brushing

125 g/4½ oz cherry tomatoes

fresh mint leaves and mint sprigs, roughly chopped, to garnish

1 Place a small pile of shredded Chinese leaves on a serving plate. Place the rice wine, fish sauce, ginger, garlic, chilli, sugar and 1 tablespoon of the lime juice in a screw-top jar and shake well.

2 Cut the tuna into strips of an even thickness. Sprinkle with the remaining lime juice.

3 Brush a frying pan with the oil and heat until very hot. Arrange the tuna in the pan, cook until firm and light golden, turning once. Remove and set aside.

4 Cook the tomatoes in the pan over a high heat until lightly browned. Spoon the tuna and tomatoes, then the dressing over the Chinese leaves. Garnish with fresh mint and serve warm.

COOK'S TIP

You can make a quick version of this dish using canned tuna. Just drain and flake the tuna, omit steps 2 and 3 and continue as in the recipe.

Egg Noodle & Turkey Salad

A good dish for summer eating, this is light and refreshing in flavour and easy to cook. The turkey can be replaced with cooked chicken.

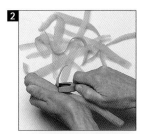

NUTRITIONAL INFORMATION

Calories 355	Sugars 6g	
Protein 22g	Fat 10g	
Carbohydrate ...46g	Saturates 2g	

 15–20 mins   5 mins

SERVES 4

INGREDIENTS

225 g/8 oz dried egg noodles

2 tsp sesame oil

1 carrot

100 g/3½ oz beansprouts

½ cucumber

150 g/5½ oz cooked turkey breast meat,
  shredded into thin slivers

2 spring onions, finely shredded

peanuts and basil leaves chopped,
  to garnish

DRESSING

5 tbsp coconut milk

3 tbsp lime juice

1 tbsp light soy sauce

2 tsp Thai fish sauce

1 tsp chilli oil

1 tsp sugar

2 tbsp coriander, chopped

2 tbsp sweet basil, chopped

1 Cook the noodles in boiling water for 4 minutes, or according to the packet directions. Plunge them into a bowl of cold water to cool, then drain and toss in sesame oil.

2 Use a vegetable peeler to shave off thin ribbons from the carrot. Blanch the ribbons and beansprouts in boiling water for 30 seconds, then plunge into cold water for 30 seconds. Drain well. Next, shave thin ribbons of cucumber with the peeler.

3 Toss the carrots, beansprouts, cucumber and spring onions together with the turkey and noodles.

4 Place all of the dressing ingredients in a screw-top jar and shake well to mix evenly.

5 Add the dressing to the noodle mixture and toss. Pile on to a serving dish. Sprinkle with peanuts and basil leaves. Serve cold.

Jasmine Rice

Jasmine rice has a delicate flavour and it can be served completely plain, with no other flavourings. This simple dish has a light tang of lemon.

NUTRITIONAL INFORMATION

Calories . . . . . . .384 Sugars 0g

Protein . . . . .7g Fat 4g

Carbohydrate . . .86g Saturates 1g

 5 mins   20–25 mins

SERVES 4

I N G R E D I E N T S

400 g/14 oz jasmine rice

800 ml/1⅓ pints water

rind of ½ lemon, finely grated

2 tbsp fresh sweet basil, chopped

1 Wash the rice in several changes of cold water until the water runs clear. Bring the water to the boil in a large pan, then add the rice.

2 Bring the water back to a rolling boil. Turn the heat to a low simmer, cover the pan and simmer for a further 12 minutes.

3 Remove the pan from the heat and leave to stand, covered, for about 10 minutes.

4 Fluff up the rice with a fork, then stir in the lemon. Serve scattered with basil.

COOK'S TIP

It is important to leave the pan tightly covered while the rice cooks and steams inside so the grains cook evenly and become fluffy and separate.

Coconut Rice with Pineapple

Cooking rice in coconut milk as for this pudding, makes it very satisfying and nutritious, and this is often used as a base for main dishes.

NUTRITIONAL INFORMATION

Calories	278	Sugars	........11g
Protein	.........5g	Fat	...........7g
Carbohydrate	...54g	Saturates	.......5g

 10 mins   20-25 mins

SERVES 4

INGREDIENTS

200 g/7 oz long-grain rice

500 ml/18 fl oz coconut milk

2 lemon grass stalks

200 ml/7 fl oz water

2 slices fresh pineapple, peeled and diced

2 tbsp toasted coconut

chilli sauce, to serve

1 Wash the rice in several changes of cold water until the water runs clear. Place in a large pan with the coconut milk.

2 Place the lemon grass on a firm work surface and bruise it by hitting firmly with a rolling pin or meat hammer. Add to the pan with the rice and coconut milk.

3 Add the water and bring to the boil. Lower the heat, cover the pan tightly and simmer gently for 15 minutes. Remove the pan from the heat and fluff up the rice with a fork.

4 Remove the lemon grass and stir in the pineapple. Scatter the toasted coconut over the top of the rice and serve with chilli sauce.

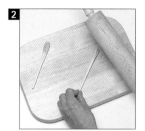

VARIATION

A sweet version of this dish can be made by simply omitting the lemon grass and stirring in palm sugar or caster sugar to taste during cooking. Serve as a dessert, with extra pineapple slices.

Vegetables in Peanut Sauce

This colourful mix of vegetables in a rich, spicy peanut sauce can be served either as a side dish or as a vegetarian main course.

NUTRITIONAL INFORMATION

Calories	249	Sugars 10g
Protein	........10g	Fat 17g
Carbohydrate	...12g	Saturates 3g

 15–20 mins 10 mins

SERVES 4

I N G R E D I E N T S

2 carrots, peeled

1 small head cauliflower, trimmed

2 small heads green pak choi

150 g/5½ oz French beans, topped and tailed, if wished

2 tbsp vegetable oil

1 garlic clove, finely chopped

6 spring onions, sliced

1 tsp chilli paste

2 tbsp soy sauce

2 tbsp rice wine

4 tbsp smooth peanut butter

3 tbsp coconut milk

COOK'S TIP

It's important to cut the vegetables thinly into even-sized pieces so that they cook quickly and evenly. Prepare all the vegetables before you start to cook.

1 Cut the carrots diagonally into thin slices. Cut the cauliflower into small florets, then slice the stalk thinly. Thickly slice the pak choi. Cut the beans into 3 cm/1¼ inch lengths.

2 Heat the vegetable oil in a large frying pan or wok and stir-fry the garlic and spring onions for about 1 minute. Stir in the chilli paste and cook for a few seconds.

3 Add the carrots and cauliflower and stir-fry for 2–3 minutes.

4 Add the pak choi and beans and stir-fry for a further 2 minutes. Stir in the soy sauce and rice wine.

5 Mix the peanut butter with the coconut milk and stir into the pan, then cook, stirring, for a further minute. Serve immediately while still hot.

Thai Red Bean Curry

The 'red' in the title refers not to the beans, but to the sauce, which has a warm, rusty red colour. This is a good way to serve fresh beans.

NUTRITIONAL INFORMATION

Calories	89	Sugars	.........4g
Protein	.........2g	Fat	...........7g
Carbohydrate	....5g	Saturates	.......1g

 10–15 mins   15 mins

SERVES 4

INGREDIENTS

400 g/14 oz French beans

1 garlic clove, finely sliced

1 red bird-eye chilli, deseeded and chopped

½ tsp paprika pepper

1 piece lemon grass stalk, finely chopped

2 tsp Thai fish sauce

120 ml/4 fl oz coconut milk

1 tbsp sunflower oil

2 spring onions, sliced

1 Cut the beans into 5 cm/2 inch pieces and cook in boiling water for about 2 minutes. Drain well.

2 Place the garlic, chilli, paprika, lemon grass, fish sauce and coconut milk in a blender and process until a smooth paste forms.

3 Heat the oil in a frying pan or wok and stir-fry the spring onions over a high heat for about 1 minute. Add the paste and bring the mixture to the boil.

4 Simmer for 3–4 minutes to reduce the liquid by about half. Add the beans and simmer for a further 1–2 minutes until tender. Serve hot.

COOK'S TIP

Young runner beans can be used instead of French beans. Remove any strings from the beans, then cut at a diagonal angle in short lengths. Cook as the recipe until tender.

Stir-fried Vegetables

Serve this colourful mixture with a pile of golden, crispy noodles as a vegetarian main course, or on its own to accompany meat dishes.

NUTRITIONAL INFORMATION

Calories 148   Sugars 7g
Protein . . . . .8g   Fat 7g
Carbohydrate . . .14g   Saturates 1g

 20 mins   10-15 mins

SERVES 4

I N G R E D I E N T S

1 aubergine

salt

2 tbsp vegetable oil

3 garlic cloves, crushed

4 spring onions, chopped

1 small red pepper, deseeded and sliced

4 baby sweetcorn, halved lengthways

80 g/3 oz mangetout

200 g/7 oz Chinese mustard greens, coarsely shredded

425 g/15 oz canned Chinese straw mushrooms, drained

125 g/4½ oz beansprouts

2 tbsp rice wine

2 tbsp yellow bean sauce

2 tbsp dark soy sauce

1 tsp chilli sauce

1 tsp sugar

125 ml/4 fl oz chicken or vegetable stock

1 tsp cornflour

2 tsp water

1 Trim the aubergine and cut into 5 cm/2 inch matchsticks. Place in a colander, sprinkle with salt and let drain for 30 minutes. Rinse in cold water and pat dry.

2 Heat the oil in a frying pan or wok and stir-fry the garlic, spring onions and pepper over a high heat for 1 minute. Stir in the aubergine and stir-fry for a further minute, or until softened.

3 Stir in the sweetcorn and mangetout and stir-fry for about 1 minute. Add the mustard greens, mushrooms and beansprouts and stir-fry for 30 seconds.

4 Mix together the rice wine, yellow bean sauce, soy sauce, chilli sauce and sugar and add to the pan with the stock. Bring to the boil, stirring.

5 Slowly blend the cornflour with the water to form a smooth paste. Stir quickly into the frying pan or wok and cook for a further minute. Serve immediately.

Broccoli in Oyster Sauce

Chinese oyster sauce has a sweet-salty flavour, ideal for adding a richly oriental flavour to plain vegetables. Try this recipe with fresh asparagus.

NUTRITIONAL INFORMATION

Calories 81	Sugars 2g	
Protein 5g	Fat 4g	
Carbohydrate 6g	Saturates 1g	

 15 mins   5–10 mins

SERVES 4

INGREDIENTS

400 g/14 oz broccoli

1 tbsp groundnut oil

2 shallots, finely chopped

1 garlic clove, finely chopped

1 tbsp rice wine or sherry

5 tbsp oyster sauce

¼ tsp ground black pepper

1 tsp chilli oil

1 Trim the broccoli and cut into small florets. Blanch in a pan of boiling water for about 30 seconds, then drain well.

2 Heat the oil in a large frying pan or wok and stir-fry the shallots and garlic for about 1–2 minutes until golden brown.

3 Stir in the broccoli florets and stir-fry for 2 minutes. Add the rice wine or sherry and oyster sauce and stir-fry for a further 1 minute.

4 Stir in the pepper and drizzle with a little chilli oil just before serving.

COOK'S TIP
To make chilli oil, tuck fresh red or green chillies into a jar and top up with olive oil or a light vegetable oil. Cover with a lid and leave to infuse the flavour for at least 3 weeks before using.

Spiced Cashew Nut Curry

This unusual vegetarian dish is best served as a side dish with vegetable or meat curries and with rice.

NUTRITIONAL INFORMATION

Calories 455	Sugars 6g
Protein 13g	Fat 39g
Carbohydrate ...16g	Saturates 11g

10–15 mins, plus soaking time 25–30 mins

SERVES 4

INGREDIENTS

250 g/9 oz unsalted cashew nuts

1 tsp coriander seeds

1 tsp cumin seeds

2 cardamom pods, crushed

1 tbsp sunflower oil

1 onion, finely sliced

1 garlic clove, crushed

1 small green chilli, deseeded and chopped

1 cinnamon stick

½ tsp ground turmeric

4 tbsp coconut cream

300 ml/10 fl oz hot vegetable stock

3 kaffir lime leaves, finely shredded

salt and pepper

boiled jasmine rice, to serve

1 Soak the cashew nuts in cold water overnight. Drain thoroughly. Crush the coriander, cumin seeds and cardamom pods in a pestle and mortar.

2 Heat the oil and stir-fry the onion and garlic for 2–3 minutes to soften, but not brown. Add the chilli, crushed spices, cinnamon stick and turmeric, and stir-fry for a further minute.

3 Add the coconut cream and the stock to the pan. Bring to the boil, then add the cashew nuts and lime leaves.

4 Cover the pan, lower the heat and simmer for about 20 minutes. Serve hot, accompanied by jasmine rice.

COOK'S TIP

All spices give the best flavour when freshly crushed, but if you prefer, you can use ground spices instead of crushing them yourself in a pestle and mortar.

Potato & Spinach Curry

Potatoes are not highly regarded in Thai cookery, as rice is the traditional staple. This dish is a tasty exception.

NUTRITIONAL INFORMATION

Calories ....160 Sugars 4g
Protein ....3g Fat 10g
Carbohydrate ...15g Saturates 1g

 10–15 mins 20–25 mins

SERVES 4

INGREDIENTS

2 garlic cloves, finely chopped

3 cm/1¼ inch piece galangal, finely chopped

1 lemon grass stalk, finely chopped

1 tsp coriander seeds

3 tbsp vegetable oil

2 tsp Thai red curry paste

½ tsp turmeric

200 ml/7 fl oz coconut milk

250 g/9 oz potatoes, peeled and cut into 2 cm/¾ inch cubes

100 ml/3½ fl oz vegetable stock

200 g/7 oz/3 cups young spinach leaves

1 small onion, thinly sliced into rings

1 Place the garlic, galangal, lemon grass and coriander seeds in a pestle and mortar and pound until a smooth paste forms.

2 Heat 2 tablespoons of the oil in a frying pan or wok. Stir in the paste and stir-fry for 30 seconds. Stir in the red curry paste and turmeric, then add the coconut milk and bring to the boil.

3 Add the potatoes and stock. Return to the boil, then lower the heat and simmer, uncovered, for 10–12 minutes until the potatoes are almost tender.

4 Stir in the spinach and simmer until the leaves are just wilted.

5 Meanwhile, fry the onions in the remaining oil until crisp and golden brown. Place on top of the curry just before serving.

COOK'S TIP

Choose a firm, waxy potato for this dish, one that will keep its shape during cooking in preference to a floury variety which will break up easily once cooked.

Crispy Tofu with Chilli Sauce

Tempting golden cubes of fried tofu, with colourful carrots and peppers, are combined with a warm chilli sauce to make an unusual side dish.

NUTRITIONAL INFORMATION

Calories	149	Sugars	.........9g
Protein	.........8g	Fat	...........9g
Carbohydrate	...10g	Saturates	.......1g

 20 mins   10–15 mins

SERVES 4

I N G R E D I E N T S

300 g/10½ oz firm tofu

2 tbsp vegetable oil

1 garlic clove, sliced

1 carrot, cut into matchsticks

½ green pepper, deseeded and cut into matchsticks

1 red bird-eye chilli, deseeded and finely chopped

2 tbsp soy sauce

1 tbsp lime juice

1 tbsp Thai fish sauce

1 tbsp soft light brown sugar

pickled garlic slices, to serve (optional)

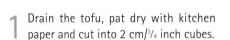

COOK'S TIP

Buy firm, fresh tofu for this dish – the softer 'silken' type of tofu is more like junket in texture and not firm enough to hold its shape well during frying. It is better for adding to soups.

1 Drain the tofu, pat dry with kitchen paper and cut into 2 cm/¾ inch cubes.

2 Heat the oil in a large frying pan or wok and stir-fry the garlic for 1 minute. Remove and add the tofu, then fry quickly until well-browned, on all sides.

3 Lift the tofu out of the pan, drain and keep hot. Stir the carrot and pepper into the same pan and stir-fry for 1 minute.

4 Spoon the carrot and pepper on to a dish and pile the tofu on top.

5 Mix together the chilli, soy sauce, lime juice, fish sauce and sugar, stirring until the sugar is dissolved.

6 Spoon the same over the tofu and serve topped with slices of pickled garlic, if you like. Serve hot.

Mango & Lemon Grass Syrup

This is a simple, fresh-tasting fruit dessert that rounds off a rich meal perfectly. Serve the mango lightly chilled.

NUTRITIONAL INFORMATION

Calories 117	Sugars 30g
Protein 1g	Fat 0g
Carbohydrate . . .30g	Saturates 0g

 15 mins, plus chilling time   5 mins

SERVES 4

I N G R E D I E N T S

2 large, ripe mangoes

1 lime

1 lemon grass stalk, chopped

3 tbsp caster sugar

1 Halve the mangoes, remove the stones and peel off the skins.

2 Slice the flesh into long, thin slices and gently arrange them in a wide serving dish.

3 Remove a few shreds of the rind from the lime for decoration, then cut the lime in half and squeeze out the juice.

4 Place the lime juice in a small pan with the lemon grass and sugar. Heat gently without boiling until the sugar is completely dissolved. Remove from the heat and allow to cool completely.

5 Strain the cooled syrup into a jug and pour evenly over the mango slices.

6 Scatter the mangoes with the lime rind strips, cover and chill before serving. Serve chilled.

COOK'S TIP
If you are serving this dessert on a hot day, particularly if it is to stand for a while, place the dish on a bed of crushed ice to keep the fruit and syrup chilled.

Exotic Fruit Salad

This colourful, exotic salad is infused with the delicate flavours of jasmine tea and ginger. Ideally, it should be chilled about before serving.

NUTRITIONAL INFORMATION

Calories	65	Sugars	........16g
Protein	.........1g	Fat	...........0g
Carbohydrate	...16g	Saturates	.......0g

 15-20 mins   0 mins

SERVES 6

INGREDIENTS

1 tsp jasmine tea

1 tsp fresh ginger root, grated

1 strip lime rind

125 ml/4 fl oz boiling water

2 tbsp caster sugar

1 paw-paw

1 mango

½ small pineapple

1 starfruit

2 passion fruit

1 Place the tea, ginger and lime rind in a heatproof jug and pour over the boiling water. Leave to infuse for 5 minutes, then strain the liquid.

2 Add the sugar to the liquid and stir well to dissolve. Leave the syrup until it is completly cool.

3 Halve, deseed and peel the paw-paw. Halve the mango, remove the stone and peel. Peel and remove the core from the pineapple. Cut the fruits into bite-sized pieces.

4 Slice the starfruit crossways. Place all the prepared fruits in a wide serving bowl and pour over the cooled syrup. Cover the bowl with cling film and chill for about 1 hour.

5 Cut the passionfruit in half, scoop out the flesh and mix with the lime juice. Spoon over the salad and serve.

COOK'S TIP

Starfruit have little flavour when unripe and green, but once ripened and turned yellow they become delicately sweet and fragrant. Usually by this stage, the tips of the ridges have become brown, so you remove by running a vegetable peeler along each ridge before slicing.

Rose Ice

This delicately perfumed sweet granita ice, which is coarser than many ice creams, looks pretty piled on a glass dish with rose petals scattered about.

NUTRITIONAL INFORMATION

Calories 76	Sugars 9g	
Protein 2g	Fat 4g	
Carbohydrate 9g	Saturates 3g	

15–20 mins, plus freezing time   5 mins

SERVES 4

INGREDIENTS

400 ml/14 fl oz water

2 tbsp coconut cream

4 tbsp sweetened condensed milk

2 tsp rosewater

a few drops pink food colouring (optional)

pink rose petals, to decorate

1 Place the water in a small pan and add the coconut cream. Heat the mixture gently without boiling, stirring constantly.

2 Remove from the heat and allow to cool. Stir in the sweetened condensed milk, rosewater and food colouring (if using).

3 Pour into a freezerproof container and freeze for 1–1½ hours until slushy.

4 Remove from the freezer, and break up the ice crystals with a fork. Return to the freezer and freeze until firm.

5 Spoon the ice roughly into a pile on a serving dish and scatter with rose petals to serve.

COOK'S TIP
To prevent the ice from thawing too quickly at the table, nestle the base of the serving dish in another dish filled with crushed ice.

Lychee & Ginger Sorbet

A refreshing dessert after a rich meal, this sorbet is easy to make and can be served on its own or as a cooling side dish.

NUTRITIONAL INFORMATION

Calories 159	Sugars 40g
Protein 2g	Fat 0g
Carbohydrate ...40g	Saturates 0g

15–20 mins, plus freezing time   0 mins

SERVES 4

INGREDIENTS

2 x 400 g/14 oz cans lychees in syrup

rind of 1 lime, finely grated

2 tbsp lime juice

3 tbsp stem ginger syrup

2 egg whites

TO DECORATE

starfruit slices

slivers of stem ginger

1 Drain the lychees, reserving the syrup. Place the fruits in a blender or food processor with the lime rind, lime juice and stem ginger syrup and process until completely smooth. Transfer to a mixing bowl

2 Mix the purée thoroughly with the reserved syrup, then pour into a freezerproof container and freeze for 1–1½ hours until slushy in texture. (Alternatively, use an ice-cream maker.)

3 Remove the sorbet from the freezer and whisk to break up the ice crystals. Whisk the egg whites in a clean, dry bowl until stiff, then quickly and lightly fold them into the iced mixture.

4 Return the sorbet to the freezer and freeze until firm. Serve the sorbet in scoops, with slices of starfruit and stem ginger to decorate.

COOK'S TIP

Do not serve raw egg whites to very young children, pregnant women, the elderly or anyone weakened by chronic illness. They may be left out of this recipe, but whisk the sorbet a second time after a further hour of freezing to obtain a light texture.

Cardamon & Lime Pineapple

Thai pineapples are sweet and fragrant, and this local fruit appears regularly as a dessert, skillfully sliced.

NUTRITIONAL INFORMATION

Calories	93	Sugars	........23g
Protein	.........1g	Fat	...........0g
Carbohydrate	...23g	Saturates	.......0g

10–15 mins, plus chilling time   5 mins

SERVES 4

I N G R E D I E N T S

1 pineapple

2 cardamom pods

1 strip lime rind, thinly pared

1 tbsp soft light brown sugar

3 tbsp lime juice

mint sprigs and whipped cream, to decorate

1 Cut the top and base from the pineapple, then cut away the peel and remove the 'eyes' from the flesh. Cut the pineapple into quarters and remove the core. Slice the pineapple lengthways.

2 Crush the cardamom pods in a pestle and mortar and place in a saucepan with the lime rind and 4 tablespoons of water. Heat until the mixture is boiling, then simmer for about 30 seconds.

3 Remove from the heat and add the sugar, then cover and leave to infuse for 5 minutes.

4 Stir in the sugar to dissolve, add the lime juice, then strain the syrup over the pineapple. Chill for 30 minutes.

5 Arrange the pineapple on a serving dish, spoon over the syrup and serve, decorated with mint sprigs and whipped cream.

COOK'S TIP

To remove the 'eyes' from pineapple, cut off the peel, then use a small sharp knife to cut a V-shaped channel down the pineapple, cutting diagonally through the lines of brown 'eyes' in the flesh, to make spiralling cuts around the fruit.

Bananas in Coconut Milk

The Thais like to combine fruits and vegetables, so it's not unusual to find mung beans mixed with bananas in a dessert.

NUTRITIONAL INFORMATION

Calories 157	Sugars 36g
Protein 2g	Fat 1g
Carbohydrate ...38g	Saturates 0g

 10 mins   5 mins

SERVES 4

I N G R E D I E N T S

4 large bananas

350 ml/12 fl oz/1½ cups coconut milk

2 tbsp caster sugar

pinch of salt

½ tsp orange-flower water

1 tbsp fresh mint, shredded

2 tbsp mung beans, cooked

mint sprigs, to decorate

1 Peel the bananas and cut them into short chunks. Place in a large pan with the coconut milk, caster sugar and salt.

2 Heat gently until boiling and simmer for 1 minute. Remove from the heat.

3 Sprinkle the orange-flower water over, stir in the mint and spoon into a serving dish.

4 Meanwhile place the mung beans in a heavy-based frying pan and place over a high heat until the mung beans are turning crisp and golden, shaking the pan occasionally. Remove the mung beans from the pan and crush them lightly in a pestle and mortar.

5 Sprinkle the toasted mung beans over the bananas and serve warm or cold, decorated with fresh mint sprigs.

COOK'S TIP

If you prefer, the mung beans could be replaced with flaked, toasted almonds or hazelnuts.

Thai Rice Pudding

This Thai version of rice pudding is mildly spiced and creamy, with a rich custard topping. It is excellent served warm, and even better the next day.

NUTRITIONAL INFORMATION

Calories 351	Sugars 16g
Protein 7g	Fat 21g
Carbohydrate . . .37g	Saturates 16g

20 mins

1 hr 30 mins

SERVES 4

INGREDIENTS

100 g/3½ oz short-grain rice

2 tbsp palm sugar

1 cardamom pod, split

300 ml/10 fl oz coconut milk

150 ml/5 fl oz water

3 eggs

200 ml/7 fl oz coconut cream

1½ tbsp caster sugar

fresh fruit, to serve

sweetened coconut flakes, to decorate

1 Place the rice and palm sugar in a pan. Crush the seeds from the cardamom pod in a pestle and mortar and add to the pan. Stir in the coconut milk and water.

2 Bring to the boil, stirring to dissolve the sugar. Lower the heat and simmer, uncovered, stirring occasionally for about 20 minutes until the rice is tender and most of the liquid is absorbed.

3 Spoon the rice into 4 individual ovenproof dishes and spread evenly. Place the dishes in a wide roasting tin with enough water to come about halfway up the sides of the dishes.

4 Beat together the eggs, coconut cream and caster sugar and spoon over the rice. Cover with foil and bake in a preheated oven to 180°C/350°F/Gas Mark 4 for 45–50 minutes until the custard sets.

5 Serve the rice puddings warm or cold, with fresh fruit and decorated with coconut flakes.

COOK'S TIP

Cardamom is quite a powerful spice, so if you find it too strong it can be left out altogether, or replaced with a little ground cinnamon.

This is a Parragon Book
This edition published in 2003

Parragon
Queen Street House
4 Queen Street
Bath BA1 1HE, UK

ISBN: 1-40540-108-7

Printed in China

NOTE

This book uses metric and imperial measurements. Follow the same units
of measurement throughout; do not mix metric and imperial.
All spoon measurements are level: teaspoons are assumed to be 5 ml, and
tablespoons are assumed to be 15 ml. Unless otherwise stated,
milk is assumed to be full fat, eggs and individual vegetables such as potatoes
are medium, and pepper is freshly ground black pepper.

The nutritional information provided for each recipe is per serving or per person.
Optional ingredients variations or serving suggestions have
not been included in the calculations. The times given for each recipe are an approximate
guide only because the preparation times may differ according to the techniques used by
different people and the cooking times may vary as a result of the type of oven used.

Recipes using raw or very lightly cooked eggs should be
avoided by infants, the elderly, pregnant women, convalescents,
and anyone suffering from an illness.

The publisher would like to thank
Steamer Trading Cookshop, Lewes, East Sussex, for the kind loan of props.